W9-BFE-769

Advantage Contractor
Business Success Series

Volume 7:
Sales, Marketing and Customer Service for Construction Contractors

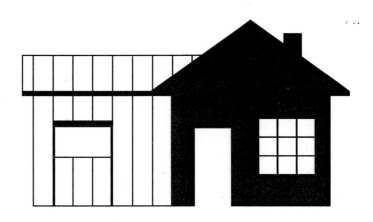

PROPERTY OF ALUMNI LIBRARY
WENTWORTH INSTITUTE OF TECHNOLOGY

Gene Fessenbecker

AEJ-7929
KINGMAN

About the Construction Contracting Academy

The Academy was founded in 1991 by Gene Fessenbecker to provide materials any independent contractor could use to start a contracting business correctly or to improve one that was operating. Shortly thereafter, the Oregon Legislature adopted a law requiring new contractors in Oregon to take 16 hours of education in "Laws and Business Practices Affecting Contractors." Gene took his information and set up the first written home study courses on the business of construction contracting. These courses were accredited by the Oregon Construction Contractors Board and still set the standard by which this type of course is judged.

Now these courses and others are available to all those people who want to do their trade as a business, as well as those who want to set up a contracting firm and hire trades people. The courses offered by the Academy through this Series allow you to start and operate a contracting business with more comfort by reducing the risk you face. Through the study of these courses and implementation of the routines and practices you can rise above the average and achieve business success in construction contracting.

Publisher's Cataloging-in-Publication
(Provided by Quality Books, Inc.)

Fessenbecker, Gene.
    Advantage Contractor Business Success Series / Gene
Fessenbecker. -- 1st ed.
      v. cm.
      Includes bibliographical references and index.
      Preassigned LCCN: 97-078294
      ISBN: 1-888198-21-4

      1. Construction industry--Management--United States.
I. Title. II. Title: Advantage Contractor Business Success
Series

    HD9715.U6F47 1998   338.4769'068
                    QBI98-451

Published by **Construction Contracting Press**,
a division of the CONSTRUCTION CONTRACTING ACADEMY
83 Centennial Loop • Eugene, Oregon 97401 • (541) 344-1442 •
1-800-937-2242 • (541) 344-5387   **www.Contracting-Academy.com**

Copyright © 1998. All rights reserved

Advantage Contractor Business Success Series

About the Author

Gene Fessenbecker, author and President of the Construction Contracting Academy, has done remodeling, custom home building, restoration and repairs as a general contractor, and worked as manager and operator of four different construction businesses over a period of 20 years. Gene wrote thirteen accredited self-study courses for the Oregon Contractors Prerequisite Education Program which have been offered through the Construction Contracting Academy since 1992. Currently, in addition to writing about the business of construction contracting, he is a dispute settler for home owner and home inspection warranty programs. Gene lives in Eugene, OR in a house that he has remodeled twice in the last 16 years.

Doing Your Part in Using this Book

We have done our best to provide useful and accurate information in this book. Every precaution has been taken to give you a product that you can use to build a productive contracting business. You have to take the information and use it as presented and do the work of operating a business, as described, to gain the best results. However, neither the publisher nor the author assumes any liability for damages incurred through the use of this book.

Special Thanks

The Advantage Contractor Business Success Series is a product of many special people. At the beginning of the Oregon Contractor Education Program Joe DeMarzo was instrumental in getting courses into finished condition. Laura Stine took many organizational and personnel challenges and found solutions. Don Sirkin provided financing to the fledgling company. Linda Seaman and Liz Overstreet made many changes to stabilize the growing business. Later all of these efforts are brought to bear on this Series. Angela Lewis and Linda Seaman made the difference as the new courses grew into being. Thanks to these and all the others who had a hand in the success of the Academy.

Contents

Table of Exhibits

About This Series

For most people who go into it, construction contracting is a way of practicing a construction trade. For others it can be a means of doing business. The *Advantage Contractor Business Success Series* is designed mainly for tradespeople who are running a contracting business. However, even seasoned business people can benefit from the information in this course.

Contractor business records from around the country show that fewer than one in five firms survive the first five years of business. Nationwide an average of 20 percent of new contractors are not in business at the end of the first year.

Going into any business is risky. Most businesses that fail do not return the initial amount invested. One of the main benefits in starting a contracting business seems to be the low start-up costs. Perhaps the ease of getting started, and the lower apparent risk, brings people into contracting who are not prepared to stay in business. The *Advantage Contractor Business Success Series* came about to fill this lack of business skill among contractors.

> "There is only one success-to be able to spend life in your own way."
> Christopher Morley

Rules of Business

Many individuals do succeed in the contracting business. The Academy believes successful contractors have learned the rules of business and follow them every day.

The rules of business exist to serve us. Often business rules have to be adapted carefully to a specific business to be of the most use. Therefore, the goal of this series of courses is to put these rules in your hands, like your trade tools, so you can use them effectively.

> All I ask is an honest advantage.

Rules of Business as Tools of Business

All tools have to be ready to use and in good condition to be useful, whether they are for trade or for business. In addition, one has to know how to use the tools well. Knowing where the tools are is only part of the solution. Using any tool skillfully takes instruction and practice.

Most of you have worked hard to learn your trade. Now you can enjoy applying the skills of your trade and take pride in your work.

The skills of operating a business are strange and different for most new contractors. It takes time and effort to learn your business skills as well as you have learned your trade. However, as a contractor, you need these business skills as much as your trade skills.

The Academy has combined information from a number of business professionals with the knowledge of contracting. We know first hand what construction contracting is about.

Money Making Tools for Your Business Workbelt^{SM}

The information acquired from the *Advantage Contractor Business Success Series* allows you to keep improving your business skills.

New information has to be worked into your routines to be useful. You will have to make room for the new, more useful information while you discard the old. This is similar to taking an old, worn out tool from your workbelt and replacing it with a new, more useful tool.

To keep improving your contracting business, you will want to keep the most useful and up-to-date tools in your business workbelt. To do this, you can take advantage of the 30 years of contracting and business experience I bring to this course. The successful use of business tools is critical to a new contractor. I can help you with your business right away by giving you specific information you can put to use today.

Self-Paced Personal Instruction

One of the easiest ways to learn as a part-time student is through a home-study course. You study when you have some extra time and where you can be most comfortable.

For an adult, self-paced personal instruction usually offers the most useful educational experience. You can set your own pace, your own time to study, and the amount of effort you want to put into the material. In this way you receive the greatest personal benefit for the time you spend.

"I am convinced that it is of primordial importance to learn more every year than the year before. After all, what is education but a process by which a person begins to learn how to learn."
Peter Ustinov

"Success is merely a matter of luck. Ask any failure."
Earl Wilson

About This Course

The Construction Contracting Academy welcomes the opportunity to provide you with the *Advantage Contractor Business Success Series* course *Sales, Marketing, and Customer Service for Construction Contractors.*

This course is one of the courses in the *Advantage Contractor Business Success Series*. A complete list of all the courses available through the Construction Contracting Academy is available at the beginning of this course.

The sales person's job is to take a wary, skeptical, fearful person, who wants to buy something, and make them into a trusted, confident customer. This process has to be managed carefully.

Purpose

This course provides the information you can use to set up a marketing plan of action for your new or existing contracting business. You will learn methods of selling, marketing and customer satisfaction that reward you with continuing business.

Because most contractors enter contracting from the trades, they have not developed the useful business skills they need to succeed in business. Marketing and selling are two skills any contractor has to learn if they are to stay and succeed in business.

Benefits to You

In this course you will be given a clear sales process you can follow to take a prospect and make them a customer. You will be given a process for marketing that you can use to develop a marketing plan of action for your new business. In addition, you will learn the means to keep your customers so that they will give you repeat business and referrals to new customers.

Through the use of proper selling techniques, a productive marketing program, and customer satisfaction skills, you can keep your new contracting business busy even in difficult times.

Organization of the Course

There are three main chapters with an Introduction and a Putting It Together summary chapter. The first three chapters deal with the three major topics of the course. The organization of the course allows you to work on each topic individually. However, all three topics are necessary for each to work successfully.

If you do not market well, you will have few prospects to sell to. If you do not sell well, you will need more prospects to get the amount of sales you need. If you do not take care of satisfying the customers you get, you will have more difficulty in both selling and marketing.

Chapter 1: Sales

This chapter details the:

- Sales process
- Elements of the sales process
- Data base system of managing prospects

We want to encourage you to see the process of selling your contracting services as just another skill you can learn. Just as you learned your trade skill, you can learn the sales process.

Show is much better than tell in getting your message across.

Chapter 2: Marketing

Marketing is the promotion of your business to the public. You have to market your business constantly, even when you have projects lined up.

You will learn to set up your:

- Marketing plan
- Marketing strategy
- Marketing tactics

Chapter 3: Customer Satisfaction

One of the largest changes a new contractor has to make is going from pleasing the employer to pleasing the customer. Since most contractors enter contracting from the trades, we will spend time on this important distinction.

Depending on your contracting focus, your customer may be:

- A property owner
- A subcontractor
- A general contractor
- A "retail" customer

A successful contracting company will have much more going for it than a reputation for quality work. It will have a reputation for building and holding a sales relationship.

You will learn to keep your customer happy without losing control of the project and without giving things away.

Chapter 4: Putting It Together

Because there are many types of contractors, it will be up to you to put the sales, marketing, and customer service advice into useful practice. While this may be all new to you, it does not have to be difficult.

Start small and simple, with activities and programs you can keep going. It is best to make a modest business promotion plan work than to try a plan larger than you can manage.

Quick Reference Tool

The "Quick Reference Tool" at the end of the manual can be compared to a glossary because it defines and explains words and terms mentioned in the text.

You, Our Customer

As our customer, we are happy to demonstrate our customer service to you. As with all our courses, we at the Academy offer our services to you through these courses. If you have questions or problems, we would be happy to talk to you.

State Offices that Provide Small Business Help

You will find a list of states that have services to assist small businesses.

Resources

This section gives you extra sources of information to learn advanced skills and gain extra advantages. Be sure to put the basics of this course into practice before going on to more complex items.

Bibliography

As a contractor you will always have an advantage if you keep studying and learning how to improve the operation of your business. These books can make a difference.

The best sales people spend 60% to 70% of the time during a sales call or presentation list-ening.

Web Sites

This section of the course will show you where to go on the net for the information you need.

Index

Introduction

Trades Person and "People" Person

Probably the hardest thing a trades person has to learn is that business has routines and processes just like their trade. If you learn the routines and processes and do them, you can be successful.

Construction contracting is a "people" business. The people you do business with are:

- Owners of property including residential, commercial, and publicly owned
- Tenants renting property
- General contractors
- Subcontractors

You have to find people who want work done and then do your work in a way that pleases them. In addition you have to work with people to solve problems.

Practicing your trade as an employee on a project normally does not involve working things out with people. One of the largest differences between contracting and working as an employee for others is the requirement that you must deal with the customer.

A successful contracting business is a profitable one. The savvy contractor wants high profits from each sale, not just more work. You can specify your best type of project and your most desirable customer just as you can specify one type of drywall or thin wall plaster. Long term business success means doing business on your terms with your most profitable arrangement.

Selling the Customer

You will not go far if you do not constantly contract new work to do. In most cases the contracting process involves some sort of sale to a person. This is true for:

- The general contractor selling a new kitchen to a home owner
- A plumber selling a subcontract to do work on a new home to a general contractor
- A locksmith selling a new set of locks to a duplex owner

You have to get people to purchase services from you. Seldom will you be able to survive as a contractor without actively pursuing people and asking them to buy from you.

Marketing To the Customer

Marketing is the orderly process of informing the public about the work you do. It can be said that without actively marketing your services, you will not have anyone to sell to. Only very few contractors can stay busy without some sort of regular promotion of their business to bring in new prospects for work.

The job of marketing your business is similar to the job of keeping your tools sharp, clean, and in order. If you do not regularly care for your tools, there will come a time when they will not serve you.

Regular marketing activities produce regular new prospects to sell to.

Your customers want you and your business to succeed. People like to be around successful people. If you are doing your marketing well and giving good service, you will have happy customers.

Service To the Customer

The two best sources for new work are:

- A satisfied customer who needs more work done
- A customer referred to you by a satisfied customer

The easiest sale and the most productive marketing is to satisfied customers and qualified referrals. Good customer service makes this possible.

In this course you will learn:

- Effective ways to sell your contracting services
- Effective ways to market your contracting services through a regular process of informing the public of what you do
- Effective ways to keep customers happy so they will hire you again and refer you to their friends who need work done

Chapter 1

Sales

Selling Your Services

People do not normally seek out contractors to do work for them. They often talk and think about projects they would like done, but it usually takes a sales person to get the person to act.

Listen to your customer and seek to understand their unspoken fears. Most people fear a decision because of making a mistake. Help them settle these fears.

Selling construction services requires that you find out what the customer wants. You will not normally have a ready made product to sell. Instead, the project you sell usually has to be:

■ Designed
■ Detailed for specifications
■ Researched for code compliance
■ Made to do what the customer wants

Too often the selling process does not include project details of concern to the owner. In the haste to get a project sold and up and going, the owner and the contractor overlook many details of the project by not dealing with them in the selling process.

The simple facts are: 1. When two contractors of equal reputation and skill are seeking the same customer, the better sales person will usually win the contract. 2. Without adequate sales activity your contracting business is likely to flounder or even fail.

People want to buy things that they like and understand. Even though they have a project that they want done, most people are unsure about buying until they are shown, in detail, that spending their money will get them the situation they are dreaming of.

Four Reasons to Buy

People are moved to buy something for one or more of four reasons. The sales process will usually focus on one of these reasons to be successful. You can ask questions of your prospect to find out which one is their main reason to buy.

1. Increase Comfort and Usefulness

Your prospect may be tired of something that is just not working for them and may want to change it. It could be a new set of stairs with a firm handrail and a landing to make the climb easier. It could be a new set of kitchen cabinets with brand new drawers, pullouts, and swing-out options. It could be a whole new house, with the room for a growing family.

In any of these cases you can work on the same goal as your prospect. You can help them gain the comfort and usefulness they desire.

2. Improve Image

Many people will buy to improve their image, especially in their own view. Someone might want their property landscaped to improve its appeal in the neighborhood. Another person might desire a deck with a hot tub and lighting for entertainment. Almost everyone wants the newest and latest trend and will often want to be first with a new gadget.

These prospects will normally describe how the desired change will improve their image. You want to be able to comment on how the proposed change would "really make the project look a lot better," and check out the prospect's reaction.

3. Protect an Investment

Repair and remodeling usually have something to do with this reason to buy. You may want to suggest this reason to buy as an addition to the others when you are helping the prospect look at the reasons to buy.

The siding is broken and falling off. The prospect wants a new image, but you can also comment on the investment points of different types of siding. The owner wants to modernize the bathroom to increase usefulness. You point out the benefits of changing fixtures as well as enlarging the shower and installing a skylight. When the house is sold, they will likely recover all costs of the extra items and have a quicker sale.

Be prepared to help the prospect locate the information to confirm your suggestion of higher investment value.

> The world's best sales person is probably the one who sold two milking machines to a farmer with one cow, and then took the cow as down payment.

Selling for the long term, when you are building a close business relationship, involves empathy for the customer's position. People want to develop significant long-term relationships. A contractor can do this quite well by taking time to open trust and meaning as a part of the sales process. You have to keep remembering the people part of your contracting business.

4. Reduce Risk, Worry, Trouble, and Expense

Many people get fed up with problems and just want them to go away. They are tired of the old and are looking for something new.

The old windows leak air and are hard to get open. They also look bad because of all the paint jobs of years gone by. New vinyl or wood windows would be just the ticket and are easy to change. They want to buy more tools for their shop, but the lights already dim when a machine is running. It is time for a new service panel and upgraded wiring to the shop area.

Find out the emotional issue involved and help to solve it. Make the prospect feel that the project will create the safe and worry-free situation that they desire.

The contract will always include references to plans and specifications. This group of documents set out the total description of the project. The contract has to match the customer's idea of what the project is.

Selling and the Contract Form

A construction contract describes the details of the project. Instead of a product the customer sees, you get the customer to sign a contract that states what the project (or product) will be.

Because you sell the project through the contract, you have to be sure that the details of the contract state the full nature of the project. A large part of the selling process involves detailing the terms of the contract. When you and the customer agree on the contract, the sales process is done. Therefore, the sale is made when the contract is agreed to, signed, and a deposit is given to you by the customer.

Your goal is to make the customer so satisfied that the sale is inevitable.

Selling Yourself

For most contractors, the trade-work they do or the construction management skills they have will identify them as unique in the construction business. Your identity, or position, in the customer's mind is critical to your success in landing work.

Price can become an issue in selling contracting projects. In many cases your identity with the customer of having superior abilities will win the day over lower prices.

Note

Do not confuse identity with image. What you want is a strong identity, not an image.

Identity is the recognition and establishment of a true situation. You have the identity as a master tile setter. Your work has proved it.

Image is a likeness or similarity to someone or something; thus an image makes you only "as good as" something outside yourself.

No matter about any other information. Get their name correct.

The distinction between identity and image is important for you to keep in mind as you seek your position in the construction marketplace and in the customer's mind.

Building Trust

It should not surprise you that most people do not trust contractors. There are a lot of stories about contractors who did not do what they said they would do. You want to overcome this negative image with a positive identity. You want to make it clear to the prospect that you can be trusted to do what you say you will do. You want them to know that your word is good.

Show your care and concern by learning about your prospect. Find out all you can about their reasons to buy. Include every detail of all that is important to you and your prospect in the proposal/contract. Let them see your full understanding of their project, and how you intend to carry it out.

The Sales Process

The sales process has two major requirements:

1. The person being sold to has to move along a line from being interested to actually signing a contract and writing a check.

2. You control the sales process. You have to move the potential customer along the line to signing the contract and writing a check.

For most contractors, the idea of selling to get work is a fearful one; yet you cannot stay busy without selling. The remedy to this problem is understanding how to move the potential customer along the sales process line. This involves knowing what you have to do to control the sales process.

The Sales Process Line

Please turn to page 23, Exhibit 1, for a graphic look at the sales process line.

Please turn to page 23, Exhibit 1, for a graphic look at the sales process line.

You don't have to be a great sales person. A good average effort, done consistently well, does just fine.

Elements of the Sales Process

The elements of a typical contractor's sale will be slightly different for each type of contracting business. These sales elements take into account the main points of the normal sales process of selling contracting services to an owner or another contractor.

The seven sales elements are:

- Find a prospect.
- Qualify the prospect.
- Gather information about the proposed project.
- Present the proposal, bid, or estimate.
- Negotiate the points of the proposal, bid, or estimate.
- Deal with objections the prospect has to points in the proposal, bid, or estimate.
- Close the sale.

Note

Closing the sale means you get a signature on the contract and collect a deposit of some kind.

Personal Sales Example

A good way to understand the sales process and its elements is to recall a sales situation you were in recently. What did you buy that involved a sales person and a sales process?

PROPERTY OF ALUMNI LIBRARY
WENTWORTH INSTITUTE OF TECHNOLOGY

The sales person likely followed a process and led you along to the close of the sale.

Note

The sales experience you recalled may have involved a sales process that you did not like. Attempt to set your negative feelings aside as you remember the sales process. Make a vow to yourself that your own sales process won't leave your customer feeling negative towards you at the end.

Moving Along the Sales Process Line

Use your personal sales example as you go through the elements of the sales process below.

1. Find a Prospect

You have to have someone to sell to. Therefore, you have to find people who are somewhat interested in what you have to sell. This is the main task of your marketing process. Your marketing process must produce names of prospects.

Of course you will want to talk to the people most likely to buy the contracting services you offer. You do not want people who have no interest at all in the work you do.

How did you become a prospect for the sales person in your example? How did you become interested in the item you bought?

Your customer is always thinking, "What's in it for me?"

Note

As stated, your marketing process is supposed to generate interested people to talk to. We will discuss marketing in the next chapter.

2. Qualify the Prospect

You have to determine that your prospect for a sale is worth spending continued time with. The person you want as a prospect has to be able to complete a sale with you. This does not mean that your prospect has to start out promising to buy from you; however, you want to know that the prospect has a sincere desire to have a project done that you can do for them.

The Sales Lead Form

An easy way to qualify a prospect is to ask a series of questions right away. The list below is an example of how to determine if a sales lead should be followed or politely refused. Never just abandon a sales lead! If for some reason the project is not for you, let the prospect know.

Sales Lead Form

Date _____   Source _____

Name _____

Address _____

Home Phone _____   Work Phone _____

Best time to call _____   Where _____

Project Type _____

Comments _____

_____

_____

_____

_____

Planned Start Date _____   Budget_____

Pre-Qualify the Project

Your prospect will normally have a lot of information about the project they are planning. You have to determine how accurate the information is and if the prospect can follow through with the project. You want to find this information out quickly.

The areas you want to explore in the pre-qualification process are:

Be a source of ideas and sources of information

Project Type and Scope

- Exactly what does the prospect want to do?
- Can they describe the proposed project in some detail?
- How much help will be needed from you for the prospect to know the full scope of the project?

Reason for the Project

- What does the prospect hope to gain with the finished project? What specific results and changes are expected from the project?
- Is this expectation reasonable?
- What will you have to do to help the prospect understand more about the nature of the project?

Resist the common tendency to believe that what is good for you is good for the customer.

Schedule of Construction

- Does the prospect realize the time necessary to construct the project?
- Is the prospect ready for the disruption to normal routines that will be caused by the project?
- Can the project be done in the time space available as set by the prospect?

Budget

- Has the prospect correctly estimated the cost of the project?
- Is the prospect aware that most construction projects go over budget?
- Does the prospect have the money or a good source of financing available for the project?
- Is the money available now?

Communication is the passing of useful information in an understandable form from one person to another. Talking is not necessarily communication. Each of you has to desire that the other be aware of how each person feels and thinks about the project. Do all you can to get face to face. Leaving notes will work only on very little items, and then not always as you intended.

Current Knowledge of the Project

- What has the prospect done to become familiar with the full nature of the project?
- Are there plans or sketches of the project drawn up?
- Is there an estimate of the project cost by someone other than the prospect?

Decision Maker for Project

- Has a final decision been made to do the project?

- If the decision to do the project is not solid, what has to be done to make it a solid decision?
- Who will make the final decision to do the project?
- Is there a deadline for the final decision?

Be clear and firm that you have to work with whoever the decision maker is for the project.

All of these questions may actually seem to be a way to remove prospects from consideration. This is true! The greatest waste of time you will experience is a prospect who wants you to work up bids and estimates, but turns out not to have a serious interest in doing a project.

Tip
Spend your time with serious prospects only. Do not bid and estimate in detail until the prospect has provided detailed plans and specifications to work from.

3. Gather Information

Once you have a qualified prospect, you want to gather all the information you can about their project. The information you gather has to deal with basic questions you have about the project:

1. The prospect said they wanted to do a specific project. Do they really mean it?

If the prospect sincerely wants to pursue the project, they will cooperate in helping you gather information for the project.

Note
If the prospect finds it hard to give you definite answers about project details, they may not have made a serious decision yet.

What is the "key issue" about this project? What is the "difference you can make to your customer?

2. Is this a project you want to do? As you gather information, you may find that the project is not one you are good at or it may be out of your area of expertise.

You have to determine early on if you might be taking on a project that will give you problems.

Is the prospect someone you feel comfortable working with? Some people are so "picky" that you will never be able to please them! Are these or other irritations possible:

- Are their children "little demons" who might hamper your progress?
- Do they have numerous pets that you will have to contend with?

Pay attention to your intuition!

Warning

One workman left his truck door open while he was working on a project. He had also left his lunch sack in the front seat of his truck. When lunch time came, he found out that the family cat had eaten most of his lunch (except for the apple)!

3. Is this a project you can do within the time frame the owner has laid out? Do you have other projects coming up that will cause problems in completing this one if you get it?

If a time conflict comes up, find out if the project can be worked into your schedule. Do this early on so you know your sales work will not be wasted.

Selling Exactly What Your Customer Wants

You want to gather detailed information on all aspects of the project. Your prospect has to clearly communicate what they want. It will do you no good to assume what the prospect wants only to find out later that your presentation includes items the prospect rejects.

The best way to eliminate confusion is to use a detailed estimate take-off process. In every case where a choice is possible, ask the prospect what their choice is.

The Academy sells an Estimating Form Kit with all the forms necessary for detailed take-offs. See the Bibliography on page 89.

The best sales people spend 60% to 70% of a sales call listening to what the customer has to say, according to a study done by the Van Volden Group

---

Formal education, type of career, or upbringing seem to have little to do with the ability to visualize a completed project. Contractors, designers, and architects have great difficulty helping their clients through this visualization process. When the owner and the designer are having difficulty communicating, the process flounders. Only more communication of different types will unravel the mystery and project a correct visual image.

Questions

Many questions may come up during the course of gathering information. These might include:

- Is the color of an appliance available in stock or does it have to be ordered?
- Can the existing foundation handle the weight of the proposed addition? If yes, who said so?
- Will the desired new locks fit the existing doors without modification? Look and see for sure.
- Will the general contractor or owner have access to the project even if it gets muddy?
- If the project gets muddy, can the work be continued? What would have to be done to the site?

You want to know that your part of the project is completely in order.

Can You Do It the Way the Customer Wants It?

The last item you want to be sure of, as you gather information about the project, is whether you can do the project the way the prospect wants it done. Doing it the way the prospect wants it done might include:

- Are there special hours you cannot work during the day?
- Are there special problems with noise, dust, access to the project, or parking?
- Is there an absolute project completion deadline? What are the penalties for failure to meet the deadline?

Make certain you have all the information before you make up the contract. An error in gathering information may put you in a difficult position if your contract is accepted.

A lot of schmoozing by the sales person implies that they are mostly talk and little knowledge or help.

4. Present Your Offer

This is it! You now present your offer in the form of a proposal, a bid, or an estimate. Now the prospect can accept your offer and you have a contract.

Tip
One of the most useful tools you have for selling a project is a complete proposal, bid, or estimate form with a professional letterhead and your business card attached. In fact, these forms can become your sales tract to take you to the close of the sale. Pictures of similar projects that you have completed are also valuable sales tools. Be prepared to offer references from completed projects.

People don't buy for logical reasons. They buy for emotional reasons.

The Sales Appointment
You want the sales appointment (when you present your offer) to be the only time your offer will be considered by the prospect. Do not set this appointment up for any other reason than the final consideration of your proposal. By this time in the process, you should have all the details of the project spelled out in your proposal, bid, or estimate.

Note
Tips on the use of contracts and samples of contracts you can use for presenting your offer are available in the Academy's Contractors Contract Kit. See Bibliography page 89.

Six Rules
Six rules will help you get through the sales appointment with the most success. These six rules are:

1. Make the sales appointment only when all concerned parties can be there.
The sales appointment is for making a sale. If anyone who has to be there to approve the sale is not there, you will not achieve your goal. Do the sales presentation only once.

"80% of success is showing up."
Woody Allen

This is as simple as following up on all of your promises for information. Most contractors won't do it.

Note
In reality, there may be some times when a second appointment is necessary. However, you should never start out making a sales appointment with the option of more than one appointment in mind.

2. Be sure all concerned parties will be there during the entire sales presentation.
The first part of the sales appointment process is to sell the interested parties on the idea that this is the sales appointment.

During this appointment there will be a decision made to buy. In setting the sales appointment, you have to find out who needs to be there and be assured that they will stay for the entire presentation.

> *Tip*
> During the process of gathering information, you might make it a point to find out who makes the decisions so you know who has to be at the sales appointment.

3. Assume that your presentation will take two hours.

Get agreement from your interested parties that they have to set aside two hours (or whatever time you need) for the sales presentation. During the allotted time you should be prepared to efficiently present your proposal, bid, or estimate.

*Customers want to feel **trust**, **care** and **concern** when they deal with a contractor. Don't let them down.*

4. Find out as much as you can about the customer's ideas of the project prior to the meeting.

This is a reminder that every piece of information gathered is useful. You have to present the solution to the prospect's construction problem. If you did not correctly understand the project and your prospect's needs, you will be in a poor position to get the sale.

Remember, what you are presenting is the best solution to the prospect's problem. Focus on how your solution will make it easy for the prospect to complete the project the way they want it.

> *Tip*
> Make note of personal items in the prospect's life and ask how they came out. For example, the prospect says "I can't meet you Thursday at 3:00 because I have to take my son Jim to a softball game." When you see the prospect next time, be sure to ask how the game came out.
>
> If the prospect says "I got a promotion, so we can include skylights and new windows in the project," when you come back with the new figures be sure to ask about the new job.

5. Be sure the project to be done is to be done now (started within a few weeks).

In order to close a sale within the two hour appointment, both you and the prospect have to want to find a solution now. If the prospect is not committed to doing the project now, you cannot sell now. You are wasting your time.

As stated, you should have uncovered this information before this time. However, if you determine that there is not an urgency to do the project, you might as well not schedule the sales appointment.

When to say "no" to a sale: 1. It was too easy. Is it all for real? Any mistakes? 2. Your customer sounds like a dictator. Everything is as they want it. If it "feels" bad, it probably is. 3. The project is too big, to small, too complicated and in some way will cost you. 4. This sale is good for your ego, but lousy for your business. 5. Payment terms will be too adverse.

---

6. Ask your prospect if they will be paying cash or how they will finance the project.

If the prospect does not have a source to pay for the project now, you are unlikely to get the sale. Prior to making the appointment, you have to know that the prospect has funds in some ready form to pay for the project.

The Photo Presentation Manual

No one ever got injured on the corners of a square deal.

One of the best ways to present your proposal, bid or estimate is to use a photo album of your past projects and other photos that are close to the type of project the customer is considering.

In addition to your own photos, collect pictures from magazines that fit the type of work you do. Use the pictures to make up a scrap book that shows variations of types of projects.

For example, a kitchen remodeler can collect pictures of:

- Cabinet designs and features
- Kitchen layouts
- Specialty items used in kitchens

Color in your presentation is useful to help the customer see what you are offering. In addition to pictures, you can use a color printer for parts of your presentation.

Special photo and picture presentation books can be put together to show the nature of the work to be done for your prospect. In addition, the presentation book can deal with potential construction problems such as how you intend to handle:

- Dust control in a remodel
- Asbestos removal in a commercial building
- Protection of the landscape

■ Removal of construction debris

Warning

If you use your photo manual to show a process for handling construction issues such as dust, debris, or landscape protection, do not use a process that is entirely different from what your photos show.

Do It Yourself Photos

You may know how to take good quality photos and have them developed and printed. If so, you can routinely take pictures of your projects and select photos to make up special presentation books for specific projects.

As with everything you show the prospect, you will want to present the best company identity you can. Be complete and professional in putting together your photo books; do not do an inferior job. A shabby looking book will not help you.

Professional Photos

You can hire a professional to take pictures for you during the course of your projects. While this is more expensive than doing it yourself, the look may be worth it.

The cost of good photo equipment is high. You may want to invest in professional photos rather than buying equipment and arranging for development and printing.

5. Negotiate

During many sales presentations there is a need to consider negotiation. This means you will often be asked to consider changing aspects of your presentation because of price or because the prospect wants to make a change in the project.

When this happens you can usually make a choice to do one of two things:

■ Attempt to suggest an alternative right now.
■ Schedule another appointment for consideration of the change.

Construction projects often require negotiations when the prospect discovers the proposal, bid, or estimate has come in different than was expected. Do not lose sight of the fact that these negotiations are

Selling is easy if you are willing to lose money. The key to good selling is the sale that's made at a profit.

Let your customers know how to get in contact with you. Show them you are wanting them to call with questions.

often just a part of the project's sales process.

Offer Solutions

You may have to work with your customer to explore solutions to some details of a project. An aspect of the negotiation part of the sales process is offering useful solutions that will point to the close of the sale.

The idea is to let the customer know you are interested in making sure that their desires for the project are met. The project has to come as close as possible to meeting their needs. You will not complete the sale if the prospect cannot find a workable solution to their problem.

The completion of the negotiating process can be called the "meeting of the minds." Negotiation helps to assure you and the customer that an agreement can be found on the details of the project. Changes to the proposal, bid, or estimate negotiated now to make the project work, will not likely come up later to present problems.

Hold up on the bells, whistles and glitz. People want interesting and believable presentations.

Tip

Use the word "you" as often as you can:

Say: "You have asked a good question."
Not: "That is a good question."

Say: "You can see the importance of...."
Not: "It is important that....."

6. Deal With Objections

Objections to the sale are a normal part of the sales process. If you do not receive some objection to your sales presentation, you may have missed something. The prospect may feel they have found a way to take advantage of you. Seldom will you find the prospect ready to buy instantly with no objections of any kind.

Your best means of handling objections is to stick to the reasons for the project as the prospect sees them. You will have to be completely familiar with the motivations of your prospect to do this. Remind the customer why they want to do the project.

"There is hardly anything in the world that someone cannot make a little worse or sell a little cheaper." John Ruskin

The prime reason for the prospect to act on your proposal, bid, or estimate is because it is the correct solution to the prospect's problem. Your sales presentation and answers to objections have to focus on how your proposal, bid, or estimate best solves the

Never take any rejection personally. You may never find out the real reason the sale didn't go through, and it is almost never because of you personally.

prospect's problem.

Answering Objections

The intent of the objection from the prospect is to present a block to the sales process because of a negative feeling they have to completing the sale. You have to find out what is causing the negative feeling and present an alternative to make the prospect feel better.

Note

Decisions to buy are based on emotion and feelings. At this point in the sales process, logic and reason may not complete the sale. You might have to deal with the resistance that your prospect may have to buying, even though they may dearly want the project. Emotions and feelings now have to be dealt with. Go back to the main reasons why the prospect wants the project and work through them.

"The price is too high."

Sometimes the prospect does not see the value in exchanging their money for the completed project. Your response to this objection should be to ask "What can we cut from the project to make it work for you?" The answer to this question will usually reveal what the prospect does not value.

"I have a lower cost proposal."

To win a loyal customer you have to offer something more than a discount.

You will often find yourself in the position of the prospect having a proposal, bid or estimate for a lower cost than yours. Your task is to review the other proposals with the prospect to be sure they include every item of the project that you have included.

After reviewing the proposals you will want to point out those special areas where you have found solutions that go beyond the others. You can also remind the prospect of the extra value of the references you provided, the skills you bring to the project, or other valuable aspects of your proposal.

Tip

When price is the only consideration the prospect has, and you are not the lowest bidder, the best thing to do may be to abandon the sale. Sometimes people who want the "best price" keep pushing for lower pricing or extras.

7. Close the Sale

Ask for the Sale

As stated, you control the sales process. Asking for the sale is the last part of the sales process. Many contractors have great difficulty with this step. Often the closing question is not asked and the sale is not made.

You may be unwilling to "pressure" someone to buy. A close is not pressure. It is a simple request to make a decision to buy. Reluctance can feel like pressure to a customer.

Remember your own sale example. What did the sales person say and do to get your agreement to the sale?

You can use closing questions that you find most easy to ask. Examples you might use are:

- "When is the best time for me to schedule the change of the locks? I have time available next Tuesday morning or Friday afternoon."
- "I have checked the weather forecast. We can start the demolition next week. Can you have the carport empty by then?"

The proposal, bid, or estimate can also come to your rescue here in helping you to close the sale. Getting agreement on certain points of the proposed contract sets up a flow of questions and answers that can lead to acceptance of the sale.

For example, you can use closing questions such as:

- "Your new locks include re-keying to match the entry door. Do you have an extra key for me to use?"
- "Your project includes two new trees near the deck. Which species of tree did you select?"
- "The concrete block company has a sale now on the split-face block you preferred at the same price as regular block. I would be happy to reserve enough split-face block for your foundation."

80% of your prospects are people who don't like to make decisions. Your job is to assist them in making their decisions.

Follow the Sales Process

The sales process has to follow selling steps just as a building process has to follow construction steps. The easiest way to get the sales job done is to follow the selling steps in order, doing each one completely.

The Basics for the Sales Process Are:

- What do you want from this project?
- How can I be of help?

A "soft-sell" is leading the customer along a series of "soft" steps to an easy and comfortable decision to buy from you.

Selling All the Time

You will find selling easier when you make it part of your normal business activities. Anyone you meet anywhere is a potential prospect. Talk about what you do as a contractor with the idea that any person you talk to could buy right away.

You may be pleasantly surprised from time to time.

Tip
Always have a business card handy to give someone you meet.

How to Blow the Sale

Don't Follow Up
Drop off the proposal and wait for a phone call from the prospect.

Talk Negatively About Your Competition
Talk about the problems and faults of your competition. People do not want to do business with a complainer.

On the average a one-in-three closing ratio to appointments held is good. If you sell more than half, you might want to raise prices.

Don't Listen
"Forget" some items on the proposal that the prospect wanted in the project. If you do not get it right now, how will the prospect trust you in the future?

Don't Prepare For A Sales Call
This is it! If you cannot get ready for the sales call, how will the prospect buy?

The Data Base

One of the best selling tools you can make use of is the simple data base. A data base holds the names of all your sales prospects. You can arrange the names to fit into categories according to the seven steps of the sales process.

Your data base can be as small as a well organized card file, to as large as a computer software program. As with all sales tools, you have to use it if you want it to work.

Index Cards

The data base allows you to keep records of all:

■ Prospects you want to keep in touch with regularly
■ Customers that might want more work done
■ People who are good referral sources that know about your work
■ Selected new names that you want to develop into customers.

Use some or all of the seven sales process steps as your index headings, and add other categories as you need to. See sample index card, Exhibit 2 page 24.

Some sales may be lost for reasons beyond your control. Understand and accept them, then move on to other prospects.

Exhibit 1: Sale Process

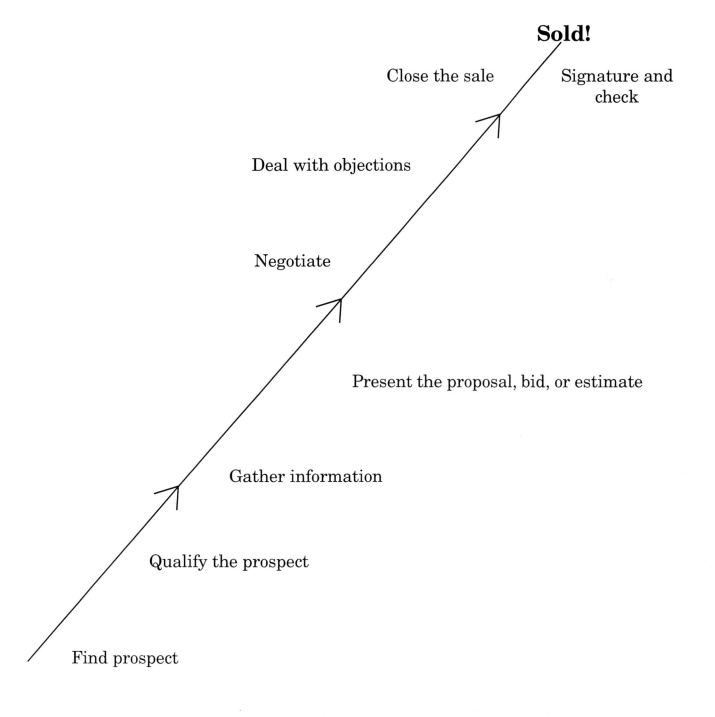

Sold!

Close the sale   Signature and
                      check

Deal with objections

Negotiate

Present the proposal, bid, or estimate

Gather information

Qualify the prospect

Find prospect

Exhibit 2: Sample Index Card

Front

Date I Started With This Prospect:

Name:

Address:

Phone:

Referred By:

Comments:

Back

Contacts:

Date: By: Results:

Chapter 2

Marketing

Less than half of the contractors have ever made up a written marketing plan. This means that if you follow through on this critical item, you will likely gain a marked advantage in competing with other contractors.

Marketing

In the world of business, marketing separates the successful operators from the pretenders. Trades people often get others to do some parts of running their contracting business. Sometimes business operation duties can be delegated to employees; not so with marketing.

You yourself have to determine how your business will regularly get new customers. In most cases you will do the activities it takes to get new customers. Marketing is how you do it.

Definition of Marketing

Marketing is all the activities that you do on a regular basis to get new customers and maintain current customers.

This definition breaks down into four parts:

- All the activities you do
- On a regular basis
- Get new customers
- Maintain current customers

1. All the activities you do

You generally have to do more than one kind of marketing activity to keep your business going strong. Subcontractors and some other specialty contractors may think that contacting general contractors is all they have to do to get work.

A well defined marketing plan should tell the whole story of how your business will find and keep customers.

The truth is that the contractor who does more than one type of marketing activity has a decided edge. The different marketing activities may all be focused on the same target market.

Unique Business Identity

A unique business identity has the edge in marketing similar products and services to the same people. Marketing is all of the different ways you can get your business name in front of prospects.

Therefore, in your marketing activities you want to do the basic things the others do in your trade, plus at least one thing more to set you apart from the group.

Excellence In What You Do

The customer wants to know you are the best, or among the best, at what you do.

_____

Warning
Do not attempt to market skills that you are not very good at. There is little you can do in marketing to overcome poor performance.

_____

Therefore, one of the most important marketing activities you do all the time is "a good job." But doing "a good job" alone will not work. You have to market your identity as a contractor who does "a good job."

2. On a regular basis

The single greatest reason for a marketing plan to fail is not staying with it long enough. Nothing you do is likely to provide an instant surge of new customers. You have to stay with your plan.

Most market plans require six months to begin to work well. It is not unusual for a good marketing plan to take a year to develop fully. During this time you have to keep at it.

Instead of attempting to do a certain dollar volume of business, look at the idea of doing a certain service that is more valuable to the customer than the competition's. In this concept you seek to gain the maximum price for your services. By adding value (from the customer's perspective) to your service you are worth more to them, even at a higher price.

Get It Right the First Time

The most productive way to market is to start out correctly. Look at this part of the marketing definition carefully. To be most efficient, what you start out doing on a regular basis should be what you continue to do all the time you are a contractor.

What you start with in your marketing activities should be what works. You will likely make changes to improve the process, but major change is to be avoided.

You are the one responsible for the success of your business. Marketing is the cornerstone of this success.

Another way to look at this part of marketing is to realize that what you do in your marketing process should get easier and more predictable for you. The longer you follow a marketing procedure, the better you will get at it and the better the results will be.

> ### Note
> Think of some businesses in your community that have used the same marketing process for years. Look at long time auto dealerships, grocery stores, department stores, etc. You can tell which store's ad is in the newspaper just by glancing at an advertisement. It always looks the same.

3. Get New Customers

This is the essence of marketing. You do marketing mainly to get new customers. To get new customers you do marketing. Do not make the mistake that when you have customers contracted for work that you can stop marketing for a while. You always need new customers.

A key point in this part of marketing is to define exactly what kind of customers you want. Getting just any new customer will not do. You want only the type of customer that is best for your type of business.

It's a numbers game: The more people who know about you and what you do, the more business you're apt to get.

For most contractors the focus on new customers is precise. You want only the type of work that fits your trade and is best for you. Carpenters do not want drywall work. Some plumbers do not do repairs.

Define Your Best Lead

What type of person or project is your best lead? This is important for two reasons:

- You want to spend your time following up on only the most likely prospects.
- You want those who refer leads to you to know the exact type of person or project you are looking for.

Clearly define the lead you are looking for so that you can explain it to anyone in only one breath. For example:

- "Sam, I am looking for people who want their kitchens or baths improved or remodeled."
- "Sue, I am looking for interior and exterior painting projects on any building two stories or less."

4. Maintain Current Customers

For many contractors, repeat business is possible and even common. Even when repeat business is not the normal situation, customers will give you referrals if you ask correctly and regularly.

If you stay in contact with your customers and let them know you want their help in referring you to new customers, you will normally be rewarded with leads for new customers.

Selling and marketing skills are necessary for any construction company to become and remain successful.

Marketing Strategy

Your marketing strategy consists of the tactics you will employ to do your marketing. You cannot use every type of marketing tactic. You have to choose which tactics you will use for the greatest benefit in achieving your market plan.

Marketing Tactics

Marketing tactics you may choose to form your marketing strategy might be:

- *Personal contact.* Some contractors can become well known in a neighborhood or with a group such as senior citizens. You simply knock on doors and talk to people. Leave flyers and other printed material.
- *Print material contact.* You may want to set up a series of flyers and mailers that you use to keep in touch with those people you want to serve. You can stay in touch with a larger number of people this way, but it takes longer for them to easily remember you.
- *Hiring help to market.* In some cases you may find professional help useful to establish your company identity. This could be just to start up or it could be ongoing. For example, you can hire a direct mail firm to plan a mailing over a year's time. You might want to hire marketing help to target times of year when work is usually slow. Contracting has regular seasonal slow times when you will have time to follow extra leads if you have them.

Strategy is defined here as an intentional plan to reach a planned goal.

Marketing Ideal

The ideal objective for marketing is to build relationships. This means that you and your customer know a lot about each other. Your customer knows you and the type of work you do well. You know your target customer and the projects they want done that you can do for them.

A recent contracting industry survey noted these results: 1. Marketing oriented contractors are the exception, not the rule. 2. Market planning and research are not a priority for most contractors. 3. Expenditures on sales and marketing are low and mostly produce unpredictable results. This puts contractors at the mercy of economic cycles and other fickle business down turns. If you follow through on a reasonable sales and marketing plan, you can gain a real advantage. See how easy it is!

Tip

People tend to do business with those contractors that they are familiar with. This means anyone you deal with will tend to be more receptive to your presentation if they know something about you. People will learn about you through your consistent marketing efforts.

"To maintain sales, your marketing efforts have to be ongoing, consistent and relentless."
Patricia Fripp

When you work to build relationships through your marketing, your customer learns why you are the one to do the work for them. You become familiar because you have been telling them about yourself in many ways over a period of time.

Detailed Plan of Action

Just as a building project has to have a detailed set of plans and specifications, your marketing plan has to provide detailed plans and tactics for each part of your marketing strategy.

Your marketing plan will tell the whole story of how you get and keep customers. Just as with a building plan, you have to use the plan to build the structure.

Note

At the end of this chapter is an outline to follow in setting up your marketing plan. Do not begin to start your plan until you finish the entire course so you get a complete picture of marketing.

Target

Many contractors make marketing difficult because they do not limit themselves to getting the certain type of customer that is best for them. While it may seem to a new contractor struggling to get started that any job is a good job, you will often do poorly trying to do work you are not good at.

Therefore, you want to be specific about who your target customer is and what type of work you will do for them.

Who is Your Customer?

You define your target customer as the ideal person to buy your services. This person has need of the exact work you do in the way that you do it. This customer also has the funds to pay you at the level you can perform.

Tip

You want to have your marketing process identify you as **THE** contractor who does the type of work you do best.

You should clearly have in mind the customer you want to work for. To make this easier use the Customer Profile Questions below.

Customer Profile Questions

These questions are designed to help you define your ideal customer. This ideal customer is the one you are looking for, the one that best fits your trade and business operation.

Warning

Do not become so picky with your ideal customer that you miss customers that closely fit your ideal. The object of the ideal is to select the market areas most likely to produce customers closely fitting your ideal.

Describe Your Customer

Residential Owner, Commercial Owner, Publicly Owned Purchaser

- Is your market in one of these groups or a small part of each group?

A strategy, when used correctly, is a force that resists change. That is, you decide on a strategy and use a plan of action to carry it out. Your plan implements your strategy through repetition.

A mediocre marketing plan with follow through and commitment works better than a brilliant plan without it.

- As a carpenter you may choose to do finish work for residences only, or you may choose to focus on installing and servicing specialty doors for all three groups.

Owner of Property or Tenant

Many contracting companies are founded for the purpose of doing commercial and public works tenant changes. This includes changes when stores change tenants or professionals change office space.

Small Projects or Large

Is your ideal customer one who wants a small item of work done, such as hanging drapes, or a larger project done such as constructing a complete building?

Some contractors want to avoid projects too large or too small just because they cannot handle certain size projects effectively.

Determine Location of Customers

State, County, City, Neighborhood

Most successful contractors agree that their best source of leads is satisfied customers. So work at customer satisfaction and ask for leads.

How wide an area will you serve? Again you may choose to do a specific type of work over a large area or a larger group of tasks in a small described area.

For example: a plumber might develop a specialty market installing stainless fixtures manufactured by sheet metal shops over a wide area. Another plumber might market full service plumbing repairs and installations for residences in a part of a city.

Determine the Number of Customers Available

How many potential customers are available in the area you want to work in? Will you have to take some customers away from other contractors to have the number you want?

There are often times when there are extra customers in some areas. This is true for disasters such as fires, storms, and earthquakes. When this is the case, the customer base will normally dry up after time. You may have to be mobile to keep up with changing customer bases.

Niche Market

A niche market is a small part of a larger market that you work at gaining control over. This means, in the ideal situation, that you will have 100% of a narrow niche within a larger market.

Tip
When you can focus your marketing energy to a small group, you tend to get the most results for your efforts in the short run; in the long run it is easier to keep control of a smaller piece of the market.

Examples of Niches in Contracting Are:

Acoustical Tile Installation and Repair.
This contractor does not do drywall or plaster. Often one contractor can tie up almost all the work in a small area by being able to be the best at one thing.

Concrete Block Foundations and Walls.
A mason contractor can build special foundations and walls with details that poured foundations can not match. In addition, a foundation mason can offer special designs and materials.

Specialized Computer and Phone Wiring.
An electrician can become a specialist in pre-wiring and installation of computer network wiring. This contractor can become known as the person to do the wiring for computers sold by computer stores. Thus, you may market to computer stores and other businesses selling computer services.

Alliance Marketing

Many small contractors can make a booming business by forming an alliance with a sales organization or the manufacturer or supplier to install their products. This will only be true if you can demonstrate superiority in the areas of:

The smaller the segment of the market you target, the greater control you are likely to have.

- Customer service
- On time performance
- Strict performance of product installation procedures

Install Products Sold by Others

Currently, companies such as *Home Base, Sears,* and other local firms contract with specialists to install the products they sell. This is true of:

- Siding and gutters
- Appliances
- Roofing
- Hot tubs
- Bath fixtures
- Kitchen cabinets

You can contact these companies to find out about what it takes to qualify for their installation programs. Find out what they are looking for and determine if you can perform to their standards.

> *Never attempt to sell, market or install products that you are not completely knowledgable about.*

Referrals by Suppliers

This situation can be worked out so that you install for general contractors as well as owners buying direct. In this case, you get referred by the supplier as an "expert" installer of their product. Usually the product is one that is difficult to install, not installed by the average contractor, or something that you can do significantly quicker than an employee or subcontractor.

The danger of this approach is that you might find times when you are too busy and other times of no work. If you can sort out how to make this type of work pay regularly, you might eliminate competition entirely.

Educating the Public

The marketing process can be compared to an education process. You are teaching the customer about you and your business. This takes time.

You have to get in touch with the customer and then keep in touch long enough for them to learn about you. The customer has to learn about you from your marketing efforts. Customers will not learn about you in any other useful way.

Tip
Remember, customers tend to buy from contractors they are familiar with.

How To Do It

To educate your customers you have to contact them and give them your message. Contacting customers can take many forms.

Customer Contact

How will you contact your chosen customer? This question is best answered by asking yourself how your target customer group wants to be contacted. This means you have to get to know this targeted group well.

How Does Your Customer Respond Best

The target customer you select will respond to your marketing best when it matches their process of gaining information on services you offer.

For example:

Remodeler. When a homeowner, landlord, or business owner wants to alter the building they live or work in or own, they will look to find someone they know who has done a successful project in the past. Your marketing will want to ensure that your name will come up as often as possible when a project of a certain type is to be done. You have to know where the homeowner, landlord, or business owner looks for information. Who will they ask for information on a contractor to do their project?

Select the identity you want for your business and then promote it in every way you market.

Telling Your Story

How can you let potential customers in your market niche know about you? What do you want to make sure your customers know about you?

- **Locksmith.** Many people buy locks or services to change locks. It is difficult to advertise enough to reach everyone who might be ready to buy. Therefore, you have to determine how to let groups you want to serve know about you.

- **Subcontractor.** A subcontractor markets to other contractors. While this is a smaller group and easier to target, you have to understand how general contractors buy subcontractor services.

Here are some basics of a marketing starter kit:

- *Business Card - Print both sides, tell your story on the back with your 35 word description.*
- *Letter and Envelopes - Get a logo or identity. Make it professional.*
- *Postcard or Brochure - Tell your story.*
- *Listing Ads - Minimum cost ads to notify the community of your business.*

You may find that helping the general contractor do a part of a bid is useful. You may have developed a special skill that is hard for contractors to find. In this way you can market your ability to do a certain task within the subcontract bid project.

- **Remodeler.** Many remodel and specialty contractors are best known for certain types of work. Some specialize in kitchens, some in additions, some in renovations.

Even though you may do many types of remodeling, it may be to your advantage to choose a specialty for marketing purposes.

 Tip

Make up a fax cover sheet for your fax machine (You do have a fax machine, don't you?). At the bottom of the page place a short description of what you do, such as:

"Your custom kitchen, bath repair and remodeling specialist."

"Decks and fences custom designed and installed for beauty and function."

People like to buy from those they are familiar with. Your marketing activities should build upon a pleasant, familiar message about your company. This occurs over time.

What Form of Contact

The key to contacting your prospects and customers is doing the contacting regularly over time. No matter which forms of contact you choose, you have to be consistent.

Whatever forms of contact you choose have to be used for a long enough time to make a difference. This time is usually six months to a year.

Advertising

The most common forms of advertising are:

- Listing ads
- Classified ads in newspapers
- Yellow Pages ads
- Posting flyers in neighborhoods and other places
- Placing doorknob hangers in neighborhoods with your message

Phone calls

In some cases you may have the names and phone numbers of people who might be interested in your contracting work. You can phone them requesting an opportunity to bid work coming up. This is especially useful for subcontractors keeping in touch with general contractors about upcoming new work.

Tip

For best results when using phone calls, make the phone call after you have mailed something to the person (or left a flyer or doorknob hanger). Refer to the mailer, flyer, or hanger when making the call.

Mail

Any mail you send has to compete with other items of mail the customer receives. You have to use an identity with your mail that is consistent. In this way the customer will get familiar with your mailed pieces.

Help is available in most cities to set up a mail program that takes advantage of lower postal rates and large print runs. Contact your local Post Office and printers for information.

With all the forms of contact listed above, the object is to have the customer become more familiar with you and your contracting business. Never believe that one attempt with one form of customer contact will get you a lot of business.

Tip

A rule of direct mail marketing is that you have to mail seven times in 12 to 18 months to build enough familiarity to produce a response. Do not start using mail if you cannot make the commitment to seven mailings over 12 to 18 months.

> Your business card should tell every important item about your business, including all ways to contact you. This includes a short description of your specialty on the back.

Know the Customer

The more you know about any single customer or about the group you want to target, the more your marketing will be effective. In many cases you could be giving information to a customer that is of no interest to them.

Testing for Results

With each form of customer contact mentioned above, you can build a test system. A test of your contact method will help you determine the best results.

A good test would be to find out the best contact piece to mail or hand out. You would have to use a phone follow up to do this type of test.

Develop two or more mail or handout pieces that will each go to different parts of a group of people. The list of people should be large enough to allow at least 25 people to be contacted for each piece developed.

Call each person on your list after sending the contact piece, noting which piece they received. By keeping notes of the response of each group, you will find out which piece produced the most interest. See Sample Test Chart, Exhibit 4, page 52.

Your Business Identity

Watch out for the "new" approach. It is an irony of our society that we celebrate newness. Yet, when you have a truly new and revolutionary product, no one is willing to take a chance on it.

The customer will view your business based on what is presented to them. All you do with mail, the phone, and printed material has to be consistent so the customer is not confused.

The identity of your business will be focused in one of two main ways:

You

Many contractors focus their business identity on themselves. This usually takes the form of a skilled trades person, a superior project manager, or a problem solver in a specialty area.

In all your marketing activities you should stay with only one clear identity that defines you. Examples of using your name for your business identity include:

- John Jones Construction
- Smith and Son Sheet Metal
- Siding by Swanson
- Sally's Unique Interiors

Your Business

Other contractors focus their business identity on the business itself. This is mainly true for larger contracting firms. Examples of a name establishing a business identity include:

- Superior General Construction
- Twin Rivers Sheet Metal
- Total Siding Company
- The Unique Interior Boutique

Warning

If you intend to grow into a large company, or want to be able to sell your company in later years, you will want to choose the business type of identity at the start. It will be difficult later to change your identity from focusing on you to focusing on the business.

A marketing plan to establish an identity that focuses on the business will be more difficult to manage. It is always easier to market yourself as the identity of the business than a faceless company name. This is a main reason to be sure you are choosing the correct identity for your business at the start of your marketing plan.

Positioning Your Business

Positioning your business is a market term for selecting your:
- Business identity
- Market niche
- Contact forms

You select the place in the market in which you want to operate. Your business identity, market niche, and contact forms make up your positioning process. You have to be consistent. You can easily confuse the customer by presenting conflicting marketing messages.

As part of a niche marketing strategy, you can establish yourself as an expert in a specific area. In this way you show the customer exactly the added value you bring to a project.

Everyone lives some where and has some kind of need for construction service.

Positioning is done in the mind of the customer. You position your name, or business name, by consistently reminding the customer who you are and what you do. If people cannot remember you, then you do not have a position yet.

Concept in the Mind

The goal of positioning is to clearly establish a concept in the mind of the customer regarding who you are and what your business does. The position of your company you want in the mind of the customer is the simple and precise identity you have chosen. In addition, the concept includes the place you hold in your niche of the market and the manner in which you contact your customer.

The good news for you is that very few contractors do any sort of active marketing that positions them in the mind of the prospect. Therefore, anything you do well along this line is likely to benefit you greatly.

You are looking for the bull's-eye. The bull's-eye is the smallest part of the target. The more precise you can make your identity in the positioning process, the more successful you will be. Spend all your money and energy projecting a single identity of who you are.

Keep in mind that you don't want to speed through the market plan. Allow up to two years to fully implement your plan. Do each step well and build a solid market operation.

A logo can be a big plus in securing a place in a person's mind. It must be simple and easy to use in every part of your marketing plan.

Physical Appearance

One important way to position yourself or your business in the mind of the customer is through the physical appearance of everything the customer sees that relates to your business. The two most useful ways the customer can judge you on physical appearance are through:

- Cleanliness
- Organization

Cleanliness

You want the customer to see that everything about you and your business is as clean as possible. Things to keep clean include:

- Your clothes and those of all employees and subcontractors coming to work on the project.

- Your vehicle and those of your employees. It is hard to control your subcontractors, but in the long run you might make clean vehicles an issue.

- Your project site. Everyone working on and coming to the project should work to keep the project site clean. No matter how good your work looks, the customer will judge you harshly if the project is constantly messy.

- Your business papers. These include proposal, bid, and estimate forms. Every paper the customer sees should be as clean as you can keep it. Use covers and folders for all papers connected with the project.

Organization

When you appear organized to your customer and to others, you give a sense of confidence that you will do what you say you will do. Everyone knows someone who would be able to do better if they were organized.

What can you do to show your customer that you are organized? You can:

- Have a file folder with all the information about their project neatly placed in it.

- Come to the project to measure for the proposal, bid, or estimate with a neat set of papers to record the information.

- Come to the sales appointment with a neat, clear, and complete proposal, bid, or estimate. Your presentation can consist of going over the points of the proposal, bid, or estimate with the close of the sale simply being the acceptance of the agreement by the owner.

- Show the customer the manner in which you will organize their project to finish on time. Give them examples of how you have succeeded with other similar projects.

Because contracting is usually seasonal, you can plan to do more marketing when your business is slow and still maintain a proper follow-up schedule when you are busy. The main idea is to keep leads coming.

Marketing Budget

You will have to determine how much money you can make available for your marketing process. As stated, your marketing plan has to keep going in its initial for at least six months to achieve good results. During this time you will have to have funds.

Contracting has normal cycles. There are the seasonal cycles for most contractors, as well as the economic cycles. Your budget has to predict those times when marketing money is going to be needed when business is not producing a lot of cash. You have to keep marketing, especially when times are slow.

Plan for One Year

To assure a positive result to the start of your marketing plan, you should have funds available for one full year at the start. You should not count on extra money being available for marketing during the budget period selected.

It takes time for the marketing activities to take hold. You may get a quick start because you have some work lined up, but to get work continually, you have to keep the plan in action long enough to get results.

Stay on Budget

The most difficult part of working a marketing plan is keeping the process going while no new work is coming in. You will feel the need to spend more on one item, or spend less on another, because you fear the plan is not working.

More and more people buying construction services are not looking for a low price. Value and confidence are taking the place of low bids as most important.

Your marketing plan has to be clear and exact. During times of doubt, you have to keep confident that your plan will work as you designed it. Most plans do not work because they are changed or abandoned before they are given enough time to start working well .

Write Down Budget Amounts

List the amounts you will need month by month during the budget period . Your budget items will likely change during the course of the budget period.

For example a typical marketing budget might be as follows:

Market item:	Print Costs	Postage	Listing Ads	Marketing Help	Totals
January	$172	$260		$100	$532
February		$80	$85		$165
March	$60	$120		$50	$230
April		$100	$85		$185
May	$120	$85			$205
June		$97	$85		$182
July		$80	$150		$230
August		$90	$85		$175
September		$115			$115
October	$100	$85	$85		$270
November		$140			$140
December	$155	$80	$85		$320
Totals	$687	$1,402	$510	$150	$2,749

This sample table shows costs by the month and by the category. There are a few parts of the budget table that show the strategy of the contractor using this budget:

Use of the Mail
This contractor sends out a lot of mail. The mail might be to:

- Keep current customers aware of the business
- Saturate a new market (which the contractor might have done in January)
- Send mailings to the same prospects a number of times during the year so they become familiar with the business name

Listing Ad
The budget shows the consistent use of a single ad medium over the full year. The contractor has identified a place to keep the business name in print.

Market Help
The contractor sought some help early in the year and then carried out the suggestions. The marketing help probably worked since no new help was sought later in the year.

Print Costs
The contractor seemed to bunch up the printing. This probably saved costs through larger print runs.

Contracting is a one-to-one business. Make your contacts as much one-to-one as possible.

Postage

This contractor pays the major part of the budget in postage costs. There are potential savings if the mail list is over 200 names and the contractor can sort the mail pieces into bundles by zip codes.

The post office has information on these options. In addition, there are mailing services that offer ways to save on mailing programs that are ongoing.

Budget Total

The total budget of $2,749 is not a lot when compared to the amount of gross revenue the business takes in. If the business takes in $100,000 for the year, this budget represents about three percent. Three percent of gross business revenue is a reasonable amount to spend on marketing.

Promote the Business on a Regular Basis

Improving your marketing skills is like raising your batting average. No matter how good you get, you still aren't likely to hit more than one in three over a long period of time. But that's great!

If you are not reminding your prospects and customers of your existence and your business identity constantly, your contracting business will be forgotten quickly by the public in spite of your wonderful marketing.

There are a number of ways that you can keep in your customer's eyes and minds depending on your type of contracting.

Flyers

Printed materials that go directly to the prospect or customer are useful as reminders. To be effective, you should assume that at least twice a year you want to be in touch.

Be sure to include the basic information and motivations to contact you:

- Name
- Phone
- What you do
- Why you are the one to choose
- Testimonials
- Photos, if useful
- Instructions, such as:

- ◆ "Call now!"
- ◆ "For free item call!"

If you can make an offer in your flyer it will usually help customers get motivated to call. For example:

- ■ "Free estimates"
- ■ "Special rates for seniors"
- ■ "Free design services on your remodel"

Use These Types of Printed Items To Stay in Touch

Brochures

A brochure clearly states the type of work you do and the way to get in touch with you. The brochure should be complete in listing all that you do in your contracting business.

Tip

Always use both sides of the flyer. Give your customer all the information you can on one sheet. You have to buy the paper, so you might as well get the best use you can from it.

Doorknob hangers

Many contractors can benefit from using doorknob hangers as a tool to establish contact in a neighborhood. This is especially true during the time you are working there.

Most printers can make the special cut in the paper that makes the doorknob hanger simple to use.

A brochure "tells," it does not sell. You follow up in some manner to sell.

Mailers

You can promote your business effectively over time with mailers. A mailer can be as simple as sending your regular flyers and brochures. You can develop a series of mailers that you send over the course of a year to the same list.

The mail list is the most important part of your mailer marketing tactic. Send mailers only to those likely to be customers or those customers you want to keep in touch with. Do not send mailers to just anyone. Have a specific reason to send any mailer.

Postcards are a good way to stay in touch with little cost. You can print up cards with your company name and leave room for a personal note. Hand written is personal.

You will normally not get the best results until the seventh mailer has been sent. The good news is that as you keep up the process, you can expect better and better results.

> ### Tip
> Mailers are best used for targeted prospects you want as customers, as well as for customers that you want to make sure do not forget you.

Phone

Once a year (or as often as you like) you can use the phone to contact those you sent mailers to. The phone call will make a big difference in the effectiveness of the mailers. You can call to make sure the person received the mailer. You can call to ask when they might have a project coming up.

Listing Ad

The listing ad is a small item placed in those publications that go to your targeted prospects. This type of ad is inexpensive and gets your name in front of those you want to see it.

When placing your listing ad, keep the size small. This ad's job is to be there when someone is looking for someone to do the type of work you do. It does not have to be flashy. It just has to be there.

The normal listing ad is a classified ad or a small display ad; often a copy of your business card.

In every case possible, personalize your mailing. Hand write addresses and use large, commemorative stamps. This is not "junk" mail.

Personal Contact

Although this form of promotion requires your time and presence, it is the best way to meet and talk to the type of people you want to work for. The simplest way to do this is to knock on doors and give out your flyer, or brochure, or leave a doorknob hanger if no one is home.

If you follow your mailings with a personal visit, you will normally have more success than with a phone call.

Advertising

Advertising is not marketing; advertising is a part of marketing. The main uses of advertising are:

Listing Ad

The listing ad was discussed above. This type of advertising is the least expensive and usually the best value for the money.

Positioning

Advertising can be used to position your contracting company. This is a more expensive type of advertising because you have to buy enough space to explain about your company.

Your marketing budget has to be able to sustain a long series of ads to create a position in any market.

Identity

Advertising to create your company identity is the most expensive of all. It takes a long time to put the identity of your business in people's minds.

Many publications will ask you to do this type of advertising. Be sure there is a sound reason for doing it and that your budget can handle the costs.

Business Cards and Stationery

Always have a business card handy to give people. In addition you should have flyers and brochures with you to give with your business card.

On the back of your business card print a statement of no more than 35 words stating your business identity. The statement makes it easy for the person to understand what you do and also makes it easy for the person to describe your identity to others.

Sample 35 Word Description

"The Unique Interior Boutique designs your living or work space to make you feel good. How do you want to feel at home or work? We can make it happen!"

Work the numbers. If you close one sale in three appointments, and it takes 10 prospects to generate every solid sale appointment, then you need 30 people to get one buyer.

Your business card should reflect both the personality and values of your company. The card should remind the customer of what you stand for personally.

Before you build a better mouse trap, it helps to know if there are any mice out there!

Tip

The 35 word statement is useful to give out to people. The statement, printed in a handy place like the back of your business card, gives anyone the ability to correctly describe what you do. As simple as this seems, it will do a lot to clear up confusion about your business identity.

Marketing Reminders:

Stay With Your Marketing Plan Long Enough for It to Take Effect

One year is not an uncommon length of time for a marketing plan to begin working well.

Stay With the Budget

The two greatest problems with a marketing budget are these:

1. When the plan starts to work, the amount of money is reduced and the plan is pulled back. This is often done because "the plan worked, I can back off for a while."

The result of this decision is that a few months down the road there is no new business. "Where did all my customers go?" You used them all up.

In marketing, as in fishing, the entice-ment is a long way away from the person who thinks they are in control.

2. When the marketing plan starts, there is a long time before it can really start working. Many contractors panic and stop funding the plan or put the money somewhere else. Usually this is done just before the plan starts working.

Spend the budgeted amount of money on the marketing plan for the amount of time the market plan is to run.

Word-of-Mouth Marketing

As stated, the best marketing is when someone who knows you gives your name to an interested person needing work done of the type you do. The goal is to manage your marketing process so that positive word-of-mouth marketing is common.

To get this best-of-all-worlds marketing situation going for you takes time and consistency. You have to work your market plan to gain the most effect.

Word of mouth marketing can be managed through a data base. Your data base should include all those who know you and are positive in their opinion of you. Contact these people regularly and keep them informed of your business. These people will give your name when asked for by their friends. This system is one of the most powerful marketing systems available.

Process of Building Relationships

Getting business to come to you takes effort. But just as it was difficult to learn your trade, practice has made it easy to keep doing it well. Marketing is a skill you have to learn. The best way to practice marketing skills is to follow your plan.

Ideal Marketing Process

The ideal marketing process for you is the one you have developed for your type of business. While you might want to fine tune the plan as you go, just as you fine tune the practice of your trade, stay with the basic plan.

Designing Your Marketing Plan

The best way to get started on your marketing plan is to develop your 35 word business description. The process of focusing on this description will make it easier to follow up with the rest of the plan.

My 35 Word Business Description:

Top sales people are more effective at finding out what their customers want and working to make it happen.

....

....

....

....

....

The Marketing Plan Outline

Describe The Customer I Want to Work With:

My Business Identity Form:
Choose the one you will use and describe how you will identify your business.

> How to get business attention: Make someone feel important. Make every busines communication as personal as possible.

You

Business

My Marketing Strategy:

Marketing Tactics I Will Use to Implement My Market Strategy:

1.   **Personal Contact to Prospects:**

2.   **Printed Material Contact to Prospects**

3.   **Hiring Help To Market My Business**

4.   **Special Tactics:**

        Seasonal

        Normal Cycles

        My Niche Market

        Word-Of-Mouth Marketing

        Who besides me will promote my business best?

        How can I get these people to promote me?

My Preferred Customer Contact Form(s):

Advertising

Phone Calls

Mail

My Marketing Budget

Fill out the annual budget form. A blank copy is on page 51, Exhibit 3.

Exhibit 3: Annual Budget

Market item:	Print Costs	Postage	Listing Ads	Marketing Help	Totals
January					
February					
March					
April					
May					
June					
July					
August					
September					
October					
November					
December					
Totals					

Exhibit 4: Sample Test Chart

Sent to

		Group #1	Group #2	Group #3
Marketing Piece Used	**Flyer**			
	Mailer			
	Doorknob Hanger			

You can use two or more groups for each type of marketing piece. Then your chart would compare responses of different flyers, mailers or other pieces between groups.

Place a check mark for every response in the correct box.

Chapter 3

Customer Service

Contracting, A Service Business

Someone receives a service from you every time you do a project. Buyers of construction services are seeking to solve a problem of some kind. What you build or repair serves the customer in some way. While you will end up producing a product for your customer such as a house, a commercial building, an inspection report, or a new set of locks, all or part of what you do will be seen as a service to the owner.

What you do as a contractor gives the customer what they want and they are happy, or it does not satisfy the customer and they are unhappy. Future work will depend to some extent on how your customers view the work you do today.

"Of customers who complain, 70% will do business with you again if you resolve the complaint. That number jumps to 95% if you resolve the problem quickly."
Jay Condrad Levinson

Who is Your Customer?

Customers expect service according to their view of how the project should go. They want to know that the work will be done the way that they want it done. Some customers want to be in on everything about the project; others want to see the work done with as little involvement as possible.

Four Customer Groups

There are four main groups of customers in contracting:

1. Property Owner
The property owner hires the contractor directly to do a project. The owner will usually be directly concerned about the progress of the project.

Usually this means the owner has:

- Questions about how the project will be done

- Need of assurances about starting and finishing times
- The requirement that you complete all or part of the work before payments are made

Everything you can find out about the owner and their desires for the project will help you keep them satisfied during the project.

2. Subcontractor

If you are a general contractor, it may seem strange to consider a subcontractor as your customer. Any subcontractor working on your project has to fit into the construction process at the correct time, with every part of their work ready to go.

You may have to arrange for:

- The owner to have an area of the project cleared
- A supplier to have certain items on the project site
- Scaffolding or other equipment to be in place

When you take your subcontractor into account as a customer, the project tends to keep moving. If you regard the subcontractor as just another worker who has to get something done, you may find a poor attitude.

Subcontractors work on their own terms on many projects. Scheduling is often a problem. Keeping a schedule going makes everyone happier.

3. General Contractor

The general contractor is the main customer of the subcontractor. Service to the general contractor will often be the one way you can set yourself apart as superior to other subcontractors.

Service to a general contractor is often given as some direct service to the owner. That is, your service to the general contractor's customer (the owner) will be a service to the general contractor as well.

4. Retail Customer

Many small contractors and specialty contractors serve their customers through a direct purchase. Often the contractor sells and installs items such as locks, garage doors, vacuum systems, and doors. In these cases the advantages of the products are often not as visible as the services of installation.

Anyone who is not customer oriented should not go into the contracting business. The idea is not to pacify a customer, but to satisfy a customer.

Your employees and subcontractors are an extension of you. They have to do customer satisfaction at the level you require. This means training and agreement on what your customer service ideas are, followed by performance.

In addition to the service of installing, the specialty contractor can make a difference in how the products are serviced after the sale. This is true for:

- Warranty work
- Adjustments to the product
- Adapting the product to the customer's specific situation

Warning

Each year about 25% of your customers "go away." Some move, some quit contracting, some stop being your customer for other reasons. Plan on this happening each year.

What Does the Customer Want You to Do?

Remember:
Listening works.

You can learn what the customer wants you to do through the process of bidding and estimating the project. The process of understanding the total nature of the project is up to you. In many cases the customer will not know the complete nature of the project (what they are really getting into) until you go through your bidding and estimating process.

Warning

Just because your customer is a general contractor, do not assume they know all about the part of the project you are bidding on. Often significant details are unknown to the general contractor because they did not get all the information they needed.

Use detailed bidding and estimating sheets that require you to ask all necessary questions about the project.

Tip

The Academy has an Estimator's Form Kit with most of the estimating forms any contractor would use. See Bibliography page 89.

Detailed Bidding

Many customers do not realize how complicated their project can get. They also do not normally understand the levels of quality available in materials that may be installed in the project.

In the case of projects where specifications are issued for all materials, there is little doubt as to the detail in most items. However, most owners are not aware of fine details regarding parts of the project that could cause disagreement later.

An important step in preventing disputes and giving the customer what they want is preparing a detailed set of specifications and project details for bidding the work. The customer can then review the specifications and make changes if necessary.

> You may have to say "no" if your customer is demanding something outside of your contract. You may have to stop and work out the issues. Your contract will become a good friend in these cases.

Detailed Estimating

Estimating is the process of finding the cost of the project. To be sure you have the full costs of the project, you have to know the details. For example:

- What is the compaction quality of the soil? Will more fill be needed to increase foundation support to the required amount?

Detailed estimating means asking questions about everything that is not clear about the project.

- Which brand and model number of locks will be installed? Are all doors to get the same model? Which doors will get deadbolts?
- Is the thinwall plaster to be the same texture in all rooms?

Including "Something Extra"

There is nothing that will give you more points with your customer than a "something extra." Everyone likes to be pleasantly surprised. In all your bidding and estimating allow a specific amount for a "something extra" in the project.

> Your customer's impression of your company begins the moment you answer the phone. You are not likely to overcome this impression easily if it is a negative one.

Tip
Do not try to select or identify the "something extra" in the bidding and estimating part of the project. Just be sure you are covered for it in your costs. The time will come along when you can give the "something extra" to your customer.

Warning
Do not let your customer know that you are going to give them "something extra." It has to be a surprise. Do not even hint that you will do it.

The "something extra" will normally come about when a customer has a complaint or a request for something that is not directly covered in the contract. Sometimes in cases like this, it is easier to give the item rather than to start disputing the point.

Do not confuse the "something extra" for the normal process of getting change orders and negotiating changes in plans and specifications. New and extra work not listed in the contract should be dealt with correctly, using a change order.

In the Bibliography on page 89, you will find the Academy's Contractor's Contract Kit which contains samples of change orders you can use.

When the customer says something really good about your work or the progress of the project, write it down. Then ask for permission to use the quote by writing it on a release form and have them sign it.

The Customer's Dream

With few exceptions, your customer has a mind's-eye view of how the project should look when completed. You have to get the customer's view of the project as clear in your mind as the customer has it in theirs. After all, it is up to you to make it happen just the way the customer wants it.

Many contractors get into trouble with their customer(s) because they do not have a correct concept (one matching the customer's concept) of the project to begin with. You have to clearly realize that customer satisfaction can only come if you understand what the customer wants and expects.

The Solution the Customer Wants

In some cases the customer does not have a specific mind's-eye view of the project or cannot express it easily. In these cases they will be seeking a solution to a problem. You want to make sure that you clearly know the solution the customer seeks.

Tip
You can often make a solid, positive impression with your customer just by promptly returning phone calls and requests for information.

When the customer is seeking a solution they often do not know what will best fit their desires. You have to work with the customer to make the solution fit the construction. This normally involves solutions such as:

- More room to store something within a confined area.
- Two extra bedrooms and a bath on a second story addition.
- Five upcoming houses that need thinwall plaster installed on schedule and correctly textured for each room.

According to market researchers, unreturned phone calls irritate customers more than anything else in dealing with businesses.

You may want to set up a "service department" within your company. You or an employee can set up a process to quickly handle complaints. A quick response and a sincere effort works wonders at changing attitudes.

Doing What the Customer Wants

After you find out what the customer wants, you have to put that desire into a form that "details the details." The contract takes care of this.

Note
Your proposal, bid, or estimate will become the contract when the customer signs it and writes a check. You cannot change the contract after it is signed without the customer's consent. It has to be correct at the start.

Detailed Contract

The construction contract has to be detailed to the extent that neither you nor the customer have any doubts that the contract states the full and complete agreement between you. Under normal contract law, the written contract will almost always exclude any

Many successful specialty and re-model contractors set a follow-up date for a month or so before a year is up since the work was done with the specific idea to ask if all is well. Customers **love** this.

verbal agreements you make after the contract was signed.

 Tip
Use the Contractors Contract Kit to develop contracts for
your type of projects. See Bibliography, page 89.

People "defect" from
a company and stop
being a customer
for a "human"
reason two-thirds
of the time. They
were simply not
treated as they
would like to be.

In the contracting business the contract is the one and only
description of how the project is to be done. Another way of saying
this is that the contract is the agreement between you and the
owner detailing what is to be done. The words have to exactly
describe the intent of the customer and yourself.

Detailed Change Orders

As stated, verbal agreements and amendments to the contract are
not usually valid. Therefore, you have to have a written process to
note new and expanded agreements outside of the original contract.
You do this with a change order.

Each change order has to detail the change, as each of you
understand it, and contain both your signatures. The process of
preparing a change order allows you and the owner to make sure
you are in agreement.

Warning
Always negotiate the change order and the details of the
change before the work is done.

Quoting Prices and Collecting Payments

One of the greatest problems for contractors involves quoting
prices and collecting payments. This is true for the contract as well
as change orders. You will often have to review your contract and
change orders with the owner to show what you agreed on about
payments.

"The purpose of a
business is to
create and keep a
customer."
Theodore C. Levitt

You have to assume the owner will not remember some of the
details of the contract. Be prepared to go over the contract and
review the payment procedures.

Avoiding the Endless Callback List

As stated, the contract and change orders detail the project.
Nothing beyond these written agreements should be called for by
the owner. If you have been diligent in working with the contract

and change orders, you should be able to keep your callback list small.

> **Tip**
> The end of the project (near the end of negotiations about the callback list) might be a good time to give the "something extra." Be sure not to use this in desperation and give a lot extra away.

Asking for Leads

The great benefit of good customer service is willing referrals from your customer. In fact, there is not a better marketing strategy you can have than planning for referrals through customer service.

Your customers will talk about you; you cannot stop them. Some customers will speak good of you and some may speak ill of you. What they say about you is greatly under your control.

People want to buy from those they can trust to take good care of them. A person looking for contracting services wants to buy from a contractor who gave good service to someone they know. Good customer service to every customer will gain you positive referrals.

You do not have to wait until the end of the project to ask for referrals. You can ask all during the bidding process as well as during the project. You can ask for referrals:

■ **During the Bidding and Estimating Process**
There will often be others in the neighborhood that are thinking of having some work done. You can ask your customer who they know of that is thinking of having work done.

■ **During the Close of the Sale**
Your bidding and estimating process produced a proposal, bid, or estimate which included all the details of the project. You can discuss with your customer how you do this process for all your customers, which is why you get new business by referral. You can show your customer that anyone has a better chance of a good project because of your efforts!

It is a good time to ask your customer for referrals when your presentation is complete and the sale is made. They may know of

Word of mouth marketing, and the leads that make it work, is based on satisfied customers. To get your customer to spread the word, you have to first keep your word and do the project as promised.

others who are currently looking to have a similar project done.

Service = Repeat business. Follow the key principles:

- *Reliability*
- *Extra Effort*
- *Pleasant Attitude*
- *Enthusiasm*
- *Action*
- *"Thank You"*

■ During the Project

Whenever you find the customer complementing your crew on the work being done, it is a good time to ask if they know of others who might want a project done. When the customer feels good about you is always a good time to ask for referrals.

■ At the Project's End

Always ask for referrals at the end of a successful project. Consider it your payoff for a customer service job well done. At the end of the project your customer knows what to expect and will be able to feel better about referring you to others.

Why do contractors lose customers? Because of a lack of interest in maintaining contact after a project is completed

Punch List Checklist

Use this checklist to help you determine that your project is complete.

- ○ Ground should slope away from house, especially at basement window wells and ground-level doors.
- ○ Entry steps are level with neat masonry work; no cracks.
- ○ Wood trim spaced off masonry to deter pests
- ○ Well-put-together wood trim; no splits or warps.
- ○ Neat siding job; no splits, warps, or missing pieces.
- ○ Paint job with nails set and filled.
- ○ Neat gutter installation, with proper slope toward downspouts.
- ○ Proper offset of joints on a wood-shingle roof.
- ○ A straight roof-shingle line along the gable ends from eave to edge.
- ○ Straight shingle line along roof valleys.
- ○ Neat masonry work and good flashing on the chimney.
- ○ Neat concrete work on garage floor and apron: minimum cracks.
- ○ A smoothly operating front door; no binding.
- ○ Wood floor free of squeaks and laid up tight, with proper joint

stagger.
- Baseboard trim hard against the floor; no gaps.
- Good baseboard joints at corners and doors, well nailed with no splits.
- Good joints in door and window trim, well nailed with a smooth finish.
- Easily operating windows with no sticking.
- Well-fitted doors showing an equal space all around between door and frame.
- Neat installation of door hardware.
- Smooth finish on all doors, stained or painted, with tops and bottoms painted or stained and sealed.
- Neat drywall joints, no nail pops, and crack-free over doors and windows.
- Neat joints at countertops with a good fit against the wall.
- Good grade of cabinet hardware.
- Neat, clean fireplace masonry work. Narrow mortar joints in brickwork looks best.
- Solid newel posts at stairways. Good joint where handrail meets newel post.
- Non-squeaking stairs.
- Balusters set into handrail and tread, not toenailed.
- Good joint where tread meets the wall trim (stringer).
- Dry basement; no water stains on walk or floor.
- Crack-free walk. Snap-tie holes filled.
- Minimum number of garage floor cracks. They are almost impossible to avoid.

Satisfied Customer and Business Relationships

A satisfied customer is the start of a business relationship. People want to feel good about what they buy and who they buy from. People will naturally want to stay involved with business people who treat them well.

Service is the key to this relationship. Service and your concern for their project is much more important than doing the best work. The best person for doing the work may be one of the worst at getting along with the customer.

How happy are your customers? Ask them about complaints they might have, then take care of them.

Tip

Whether you contract a project or not, you can send a thank you note for any of these reasons:

- Opportunity to bid the project
- For choosing you to do the project
- Patience during a difficult part of the project

Be the best at customer service. You can always hire the best crafts person to do the work.

Reminders:

In many ways the American customer has a "spoiled brat" type of attitude. They want exactly the product they imagine, in the way they want it, and "do it now." If you think you can avoid these folks, think again.

- Return calls promptly. Treat all your clients with respect and concern; your clients are your livelihood!
- Be on time for appointments, with proposals, bids, and estimates, and with completion of the project. If problems cause delays, immediately call your clients to explain and reschedule.
- Let the customer know right away of any change in schedules, materials, and deliveries. Communication is one of your most important customer service tools. For Example:

  - Let your customer know how long the electricity or water service will be off.
  - When will the new window coverings be delivered?
  - How much of a mess will the drywall installers make, and who has to clean it up?
  - When will the new locks be installed?
  - When will the bedroom paint be dry enough to move furniture back in?
  - When can they walk on the newly installed vinyl flooring in the kitchen?

These may be minor questions to you, but they are of major concern to your customer!

Chapter 4

Putting It Together

Sales, marketing, and customer service can work together to keep your business growing and strong. Your business exists as an identity in the mind of the customer. In all cases this identity is based on the customer's experience with you. You select the identity you want and put your company identity in the mind of the customer.

Every aspect of your sales, marketing, and customer service activities builds the customer identity of you and your business. It will be positive or negative as you manage it to be.

There is no reason to be "bullied" by a customer. Realize that in a few difficult cases you will have a problem. Do what the contract says and firmly hold to your position.

Long Term View

The key to dealing with plans for sales, marketing, and customer service is to take the long view. Your choices have to be considered for their long term effects. Focusing your efforts consistently in a single direction will more likely produce the business identity you desire.

You do not want to be constantly starting something new in sales and marketing. Take the time at the beginning to find the correct sales and marketing process for you. In this way you will save the greatest time and money as you get your sales, marketing, and customer service systems going.

Sales

Customers do not normally seek out contractors for work; you have to find a prospect and make a sale. Depending on the nature of the work you do, the sale may be easy or hard. You may have to make a lot of sales every year, or just a few, depending on the nature of your business.

No matter the situation, you have to sell your work. Getting the sale is the end of a successful marketing process.

Marketing

Marketing is all of the activities that you do regularly to get new business. Your marketing activity produces prospects that you can present bids and estimates to. These prospects have to be coming along regularly. In addition to doing your work and selling new projects, you have to keep new names coming up.

Make the Most of Your Satisfied Customers

Marketing is easier when past customers refer new prospects to you. As discussed in Chapter 3: Customer Service, there is no more effective and inexpensive way to market than to sell to repeat customers and gain referrals from them. It is impossible to successfully market and get referrals from dissatisfied customers.

"The question of who is right and who is wrong misses the heart of true customer relations. The issue is how am I treated, not whether I am right or wrong."
Lorne Bostwick

Quick Reference Tool

Bid
A document stating the nature of work to be done in written detail including the price. The bid might not include a contract form, but has an area for the acceptance of the price and specifications for the work to be done.

Brochures
The promotion pieces you use to make detailed descriptions of your business with information beyond that of flyers. The brochure is a complete selling aid.

Business Identity
The specific way you want people to perceive your business. The mental and physical concept you want your prospect to have of your business.

Close
The act of completing the sale. In contracting this takes the form of a signature on the contract and a check for a deposit.

Customer Contact
The methods you choose to contact your customers. These include mail, phone, and personal calls.

Customer Profile
The description of your preferred customer. Someone who fits the type of person you want to do work for.

Customer's Dream
The customer's idea of how their project should go. The idea in the customer's mind of the finished project. The ideal you have to match for maximum customer satisfaction.

Data Base
The list of prospects and customers you keep for the purpose of staying in contact and recording the results of those contacts. A card file or other organized list.

Decision Maker

The person who will make the decision to do the project. This is the person who has to be present at the sales appointment, all during the sales presentation, and through the close of the sale.

Doorknob Hangers

A type of flyer you can leave on a prospect's doorknob when you personally call on houses in a neighborhood. Use this when the prospect is not home.

Estimate

A document stating a price for certain work to be done. Usually an estimate is for a small project and can be signed to form a contract. The estimate is often changed to include or exclude work before it is signed.

Flyers

The business promotion pieces you make up to hand out or post.

Gather Information

The process of making sure you have every piece of important information you need to make a complete proposal, bid, or estimate.

Listing Ad

A small classified or display ad having the purpose of keeping your business name in front of your prospect's eyes.

Mailers

A set of printed promotion pieces sent by mail to prospects. You can use the same promotion pieces in your mailers that you made up for your flyers and brochures.

Market

All the activities that you do on a regular basis to get new customers and maintain current customers.

Marketing

The orderly process of informing the public about the work you do.

Marketing Budget

The amount of business funds you set aside exclusively for marketing. The budget period for the marketing budget is usually six months to a year.

Marketing Ideal

Build relationships with prospects and customers to keep new business coming in. Usually done through use of the marketing plan.

Marketing Plan

A detailed written process listing the marketing activities and tactics you will use to present your business identity to the public.

Marketing Strategy

The group of tactics you choose to implement your marketing plan.

Marketing Tactics

The specific marketing activities you do to get prospects to choose your business for their project.

Negotiate

Work with the prospect to solve problems and seek solutions to difficult parts of the project. Often the prospect will change aspects of the project to save money or improve a part of the project.

Niche Market

The small part of a larger market where you can seek to get up to 100% of the business available. Your business identity may include the niche you focus on.

Objection

The part of the sales process when the prospect has questions about the decision to complete the sale. Usually the prospect is experiencing fear of making the decision and presents objections to completing the sale.

Physical Appearance

The part of your business the prospect sees. Included are your vehicle, your clothes, your forms and papers, and your business organization.

Positioning

The process of getting your desired business identity into the mind of the prospect.

Pre-qualify the Project

Part of qualifying the prospect. You determine that the prospect knows what is to be done, and will not abandon the project because of small problems that come up during the bidding of the project or while arranging financing for the project.

Proposal

A document stating in writing the complete nature of a project, written so that when accepted by the prospect with a signature, a contract is formed.

Prospect

A person who may be interested in having you do work for them.

Qualified Referral

The name of a person given to you that is definitely interested in the work you do. Usually this person has a project in mind to do and is looking for someone to do it.

Qualify the Prospect

Determining that the prospect is ready to have some work done. You want to know before you put a lot of work into a proposal, bid, or estimate that the work is likely to be done.

Referral

The name of a person given to you by someone else. Usually someone who is a prospect for you.

Sale Process Line

A process of finding a prospect and leading the prospect through the sales process to the close of the sale.

Sales Appointment

The time when all parties that are needed to complete the sale are together. The object of the sales appointment is to close the sale.

Sales Elements

There are seven sales elements to the sales process:

- Find a prospect
- Qualify the prospect
- Gather Information about the proposed project
- Present the proposal, bid, or estimate
- Negotiate the points of the proposal, bid, or estimate
- Deal with objections from the prospect

Sales Presentation

The time when you present your proposal, bid, or estimate. Usually the sales presentation is done at the sales appointment.

Sell

The process of taking a prospect through a series of steps starting with a general interest by the prospect through the close of the sale.

Something Extra

The extra work or detail you save to give the customer when appropriate. Usually this is done when negotiating at the end of the project, or to maintain your business identity of giving "something extra."

Word-of-Mouth Marketing

The most efficient use of marketing. Getting people to recommend you to others.

You, Our Customer

As our customer, we are happy to demonstrate our customer service to you. As with all our courses, we at the Academy offer our services to you through these courses. If you have questions or problems, we would be happy to talk to you.

We ask that you follow this process:

1. Read the course and check out the Bibliography for more leads on your question. If you have a library available, you can check out the books or ask the librarian how to find them. Please check at least one resource before contacting us.

2. Frame your question(s) on paper before contacting us. You will find it very useful to write your question down. In this way you make sure you know exactly what you want to ask.

3. Our first response to your question will usually be to refer you to other courses in the Advantage Contractor Business Success Series, or Resources in the courses. We want you to learn how to find information on your own. Developing skill at finding information gives you a powerful advantage as a contractor. If you rely on us for your information, you are limited and become dependent on us. Remember, you are an **independent** construction contractor.

4. If, after looking for information on your own, you still have a question, please contact us. We assume at this point that your question will now be more detailed, having gathered some information. However, we may still refer you to a specific source which will answer your question. The object of this process will be similar to what a teacher would do in assisting you to learn how to ask informed questions and find new sources of answers.

How to contact us in order of our preference:

A. E-Mail: Info@Contracting-Academy.com

B. Fax inquiry: 541-344-5387

C. US Mail: 83 Centennial Loop, Eugene, OR 97401

D. Phone: 541-344-1442

Thanks for your cooperation in following this process.

State Offices That Provide Small Business Help

Alabama
Alabama Development Office
State Capitol
Montgomery, AL 36130
(800) 248-0333* (205) 263-0048

Alaska
Division of Economic Development
Department of Commerce and Economic
  Development
PO Box D
Juneau, AK 99811
(907) 465-2017

Arizona
Office of Business Finance
Department of Commerce
3800 North Central Avenue
Suite 1500
Phoenix, AZ 85012
(602) 280-1341

Arkansas
Small Business Information Center
Industrial Development Commission
State Capitol Mall
Room 4C-300
Little Rock, AR 72201
(501) 682-5275

California
Office of Small Business
Department of Commerce
801 K Street, Suite 1700
Sacramento, CA 95814
(916) 327-4357 (916) 445-6545

Colorado
One-Stop Assistance Center
1560 Broadway, Suite 1530
Denver, CO 80202
(800) 333-7798 (303) 592-5920

Connecticut
Small Business Services
Department of Economic Development
865 Brook Street
Rocky Hill, CN 06067
(203) 258-4269

Delaware
Development Office
PO Box 1401
99 Kings Highway
Dover, DE 19903
(302) 736-4271

District of Columbia
Office of Business and Economic
  Development
Tenth Floor
717 14th Street NW
Washington, DC 20005
(202) 727-6600

Florida
Bureau of Business Assistance
Department of Commerce
107 West Gaines Street, Room 443
Tallahassee, FL 32399-2000
(800) 342-0771*

* In state calling only

Georgia

Department of Community Affairs
100 Peachtree Street, Suite 1200
Atlanta, GA 30303
(404) 656-6200

Hawaii

Small Business Information Service
737 Bishop Street, Suite 1900
Honolulu, HI 96813
(808) 578-7645 (808) 543-6691

Idaho

Economic Development Division
Department of Commerce
700 State Street
Boise, ID 83720-2700
(208) 334-2470

Illinois

Small Business Assistance Bureau
Department of Commerce and
    Community Affairs
620 East Adams Street
Springfield, IL 62701
(800) 252-2923*

Indiana

Ombudsman's Office
Business Development Division
Department of Commerce
One North Capitol, Suite 700
Indianapolis, IN 46204-2288
(800) 824-2476* (317) 232-7304

Iowa

Bureau of Small Business Development
Department of Economic Development
200 East Grand Avenue
Des Moines, IA 50309
(800) 532-1216* (515) 242-4899

Kansas

Division of Existing Industry
Development
400 SW Eighth Street
Topeka, KS 66603
(785) 296-5298

Kentucky

Division of Small Business
Capitol Plaza Tower
Frankfort, KY 40601
(800) 626-2250* (502) 564-4252

Louisiana

Development Division
Office of Commerce and Industry
PO Box 94185
Baton Rouge, LA 70804-9185
(504) 342-5365

Maine

Business Development Division
State Development Office
State House
Augusta, ME 04333
(800) 872-3838* (207) 289-3153

Maryland

Division of Business Development
Department of Economic and
Employment Development
217 East Redwood Street
Baltimore, MD 21202
(800) 873-7232 (301) 333-6996

Massachusetts

Office of Business Development
100 Cambridge Street
13th Floor
Boston, MA 02202
(617) 727-3206

* In state calling only

Michigan
Michigan Business Ombudsman
Department of Commerce
PO Box 30107
Lansing, MI 48909
(800) 232-2727* (517) 373-6241

Minnesota
Small Business Assistance Office
Department of Trade and Economic
    Development
900 American Center Building
150 East Kellogg Boulevard
St. Paul, MN 55101
(800) 652-9747 (612) 296-3871

Mississippi
Small Business Bureau
Research and Development Center
PO Box 849
Jackson, MS 39205
(601) 359-3552

Missouri
Small Business Bureau
Research and Development Center
PO Box 118
Jefferson City, MO 65102
(314) 751-4982 (314) 751-8411

Montana
Business Assistance Division
Department of Commerce
1424 Ninth Ave.
Helena, MT 59620
(800) 221-8015* (406) 444-2801

Nebraska
Existing Business Division
Department of Economic Development
PO Box 94666
301 Centennial Mall South
Lincoln, NE 68509-4666
(402) 471-3782

Nevada
Nevada Commission of Economic
    Development
Capitol Complex
Carson City, NV 89710
(702) 687-4325

New Hampshire
Small Business Development Center
University Center
400 Commercial Street, Room 311
Manchester, NH 03101
(603) 625-4522

New Jersey
Office of Small Business Assistance
Department of Commerce and Economic
    Development
20 West State Street, CN 835
Trenton, NJ 08625
(609) 984-4442

New Mexico
Economic Development Division
Department of Economic Development
1100 St. Francis Drive
Santa Fe, NM 87503
(505) 827-0300

New York
Division for Small Business
Department of Economic Development
1515 Broadway
51st Floor
New York, NY 10036
(212) 827-6150

North Carolina
Small Business Development Division
Department of Economic and
Community Development
Dobbs Building, Room 2019
430 North Salisbury Street
Raleigh, NC 27611
(919) 733-2810

* In state calling only

North Dakota
Small Business Coordinator
Economic Development Commission
Liberty Memorial Building
604 East Boulevard
Bismark, ND 58505
(701) 224-2810

Ohio
Small and Developing Business Division
Department of Development
PO Box 1001
Columbus, OH 43266-0101
(800) 248-4040* (614) 466-4232

Oklahoma
Oklahoma Department of Commerce
PO Box 26980
6601 N. Broadway Extension
Oklahoma City, OK 73126-0980
(800) 477-6552* (405) 843-9770

Oregon
Economic Development Department
775 Summer Street NE
Salem, OR 97310
(800) 233-3306* (503) 373-1200

Pennsylvania
Bureau of Small Business and
    Appalachian Development
Department of Commerce
461 Forum Building
Harrisburg, PA 17120
(717) 783-5700

Puerto Rico
Commonwealth Department of
    Commerce
Box S
4275 Old San Juan Station
San Juan, PR 00905
(809) 721-3290

Rhode Island
Business Development Division
Department of Economic Development
Seven Jackson Walkway
Providence, RI 02903
(401) 277-2601

South Carolina
Enterprise Development
PO Box 1149
Columbia, SC 29202
(800) 922-6684* (803) 737-0888

South Dakota
Governor's Office of Economic
    Development
Capital Lake Plaza
711 Wells Avenue
Pierre, SD 57501
(800) 872-6190* (605) 773-5032

Tennessee
Small Business Office
Department of Economic and
Community Development
320 Sixth Avenue North
Seventh Floor
Rachel Jackson Building
Nashville, TN 37219
(800) 872-7201* (615) 741-2626

Texas
Small Building Division
Department of Commerce
Economic Development Commission
PO Box 12728
Capitol Station
410 East Fifth Street
Austin, TX 78711
(800) 888-0511 (512) 472-5059

* In state calling only

Utah

Small Business Development Center
102 West 500 South, Suite 315
Salt Lake City, UT 84101
(801) 581-7905

Vermont

Agency of Development and Community
   Affairs
The Pavilion
109 State Street
Montpelier, VT 05609
(800) 622-4553* (802) 828-3221

Virginia

Small Business and Financial Services
Department of Economic Development
PO Box 798
1000 Washington Building
Richmond, VA 23206
(804) 371-8252

Washington

Small Business Development Center
245 Todd Hall
Washington State University
Pullman, WA 99164-4727
(509) 335-1576

West Virginia

Small Business Development Center
   Division
1115 Virginia Street East
Charleston, WV 25301
(304) 348-2960

Wisconsin

Public Information Bureau
Department of Development
PO Box 7970
123 West Washington Avenue
Madison, WI 53707
(800) 435-7287* (608) 266-1018

Wyoming

Economic Development and
Stabilization Board
Herschler Building
Cheyenne, WY 82002
(307) 777-7287

* In state calling only
Source: National Association for the Self-
Employed,
USA TODAY research

Resources

The following sources are generally recognized as associated members of the building industry that have impact on standards and guidelines of business operations. You can contact these sources to get specific information on products and business ideas in your specific trade or business area. In some cases you can go to a local chapter for help. These associations will be promoting their product or service, but will also be able to answer many business, technical and product questions.

Air Conditioning Contractors of America (ACCA)
1513 16th St. NW
Washington, DC 20036

Air Conditioning and Refrigeration Institute
4301 N. Fairfax Dr. Suite 425
Arlington, VA 22203
(703) 524-8800

Aluminum Association (AA)
900 19th St. NW, Ste. 300
Washington, DC 20006
(202) 862-5100

American Association of Nurserymen
1250 I St. NW, Suite 500
Washington, DC 20005
(202) 789-2900

American Building Contractors Assn.
PO Box 2772
Cypress, CA 90630
(714) 828-4760
http://www.netcom.com/~w-e/abca.html

American Concrete Institute (ACI)
P.O. Box 19150
Detroit, MI 48219

American Gas Association
1515 Wilson Blvd.
Arlington, VA 22209
(703) 841-8589

American Hardboard Association
520 N. Hicks Rd.
Palatine, IL 60067
(312) 934-8800

American Hardware Manufacturers Association (AHMA)
801 N. Plaza Drive
Schaumburg, IL 60173-4977
(847) 605-1025

American Institute of Building Design
991 Post Rd. E.
Westport, CT 06880
(800) 366-2423

American Institute of Steel Construction, Inc.
1 E. Wacker Dr., Ste. 3100
Chicago, IL 60601-2001
(312) 670-2400

American Institute of Timber Construction (AITC)
11818 SE Mill Plain Blvd., Ste. 415
Vancouver, WA 98684
(206) 254-9132

American Insurance Association (AIA)
1130 Connecticut Ave. NW, Ste. 1000
Washington, DC 20036
(202) 828-7100

American Iron and Steel Institute (AISI)
1133 15th St. NW
Washington, DC 20005
(202) 452-7100

America Lighting Association
World Trade Center
PO Box 420288
Dallas, TX 75342-0288
(800) 605-4448

American National Standards Institute (ANSI)
11 W. 42nd St., 13th floor
New York, NY 10036
(212) 642-4900

American Plywood Association (APA)
P.O. Box 11700
Tacoma, WA 98411
(206) 565-6600

American Society of Heating, Refrigeration and Air Conditioning Engineers
1791 Tullie Circle NE
Atlanta, GA 30329
(404) 636-8400

American Society of Home Inspectors
85 W. Algonquin Rd., Suite 360
Arlington Heights, IL 60005
(800) 743-ASHI (2744)

American Society of Interior Designers
608 Massachusetts Ave. NW
Washington, DC 20002-6006
(202) 546-3480

American Society of Testing Materials (ASTM)
100 Bar Harbor Dr.
West Conshohocken, PA 19428-2959
(610) 832-9500

American Solar Energy Society (ASES)
2400 Central Ave. Suite G1
Boulder, CO 80301
(303) 443-3130

American Subcontractors Association
1004 Duke St.
Alexandria, VA 22314
(703) 684-3450
ASAoffice@aol.com

American Welding Society, Inc. (AWS)
550 LeJeune Rd. NW, P.O. Box 351040
Miami, FL 33135
(305) 443-9353

American Wood-Preservers Association (AWPA)
P.O. Box 286
Woodstock, MD 21163-0286
(410) 465-3169

American Wood Preservers Bureau (AWPB)
P.O. Box 5283
Springfield, VA 22150
(703)339-6660

American Wood Preservers Institute (AWPI)
1945 Old Gallows Rd., Ste. 550
Vienna, VA 22182

Appraisal Institute
875 N. Michigan Ave. Suite 2400
Chicago, IL 60611-1980
(312) 335-4100

Architectural Woodwork Institute
  13924 Braddock Rd. Suite 100
  Centreville, VA 22020-1910
  (703) 222-1100

Asphalt Roofing Manufacturers
  6288 Montrose Rd.
  Rockville, MD 20852
  (301) 231-9050

Association for Preservation Technology
  PO Box 3511
  Williamsburgh, VA 23187
  (703) 373-1621

Association for Safe & Accessible Products
  1511 K. St., N. W., Suite 600
  Washington, OR 20005-4905
  (202) 347-8200
  asapdc@aol.com

Association of Construction Inspectors
  8383 E. Evans St.
  Scottsdale, AZ 85260
  (602) 998-8021
  aci@iami.org
  http://iami.org/aci.html

Association of Home Appliance Manufacturers
  20 N. Wacker Dr.
  Chicago, IL 60606-2806
  (312) 984-5800

Brick Institute of America (BIA)
  11490 Commerce Park Dr.
  Reston, VA 22091
  (703) 620-0010

Building Systems Councils of NAHB
  15th & M Streets NW
  Washington, DC 20005

Canadian Home Builders' Association
  150 Laurier Ave. W. Suite 200
  Ottawa, ON K1P 5J4 Canada
  (613) 230-3060

Canadian Retail Hardware Association (CRHA)
  6800 Campobello Rd.
  Mississauga, ON L5N 2L8 Canada
  (905) 821-3470

The Carpet and Rug Institute
  PO Box 2049
  Dalton, GA 30722-2048
  (706) 278-3176

Cast Iron Soil Pipe Institute
  5939 Shallowford Rd. Suite 419
  Chattanooga, TN 37421
  615-892-0137

Cedar Shake and Shingle Bureau
  515 116th Ave. NW, Ste. 275
  Bellevue, WA 98004-5294
  (206) 453-1323

Cellulose Insulation Manufacturers Association
  136 S. Keowee St.
  Dayton, OH 45402
  (513) 222-2464
  assocoffice@delphi.com
  ah803@dayton.wright.edu

Ceramic Tile Institute of America
  800 Roosevelt Rd. Bldg C, Suite 20
  Glen Ellyn, IL 60137
  (708) 545-9415

Concrete Reinforcing Steel Institute (CRSI)
  933 Plum Grove Rd.
  Schaumburg, IL 60173

Decorative Laminate Products Association
13924 Braddock Rd., Suite 100
Centreville, VA 22020
(800) 684-3572

Energy Efficiency and Renewable Energy Clearinghouse (EREC)
PO Box 3048
Merrifield, VA 22116
(800) 363-3732
doe.erec@nciinc.com
http://www.erecbbs.nciinc.com

The Environmental Information Assn.
4915 Auburn Ave., Suite 303
Bethesda, MD 20814
(301) 961-4999

Forest Products Research Society
2801 Marshall Court
Madison, WI 53705
(608) 231-1361

Garage Door Hardware Association
2850 S. Ocean Blvd., Suite 311
Palm Beach, FL 33480-5535
(407) 533-0991

Gypsum Association (GA)
810 1st St. NE, Suite 510
Washington, DC 20002
(202) 289-5440

Hardwood Plywood Manufacturer's Association (HPMA)
1825 Michael Faraday Dr., P.O. Box 2789
Reston, VA 22090

Home Automation Association
808 17th St. NW, Suite 200
Washington, DC 20006-3910
(202) 223-9669
75250.1274@copuserve.com

Home Fashion Products Association
355 Lexington Ave. 17th Fl.
New York, NY 10017-6603

Home Improvement Research Institute
400 Knightsbridge Pkwy
Lincolnshire, IL 60069-3646
847-634-4368

Home Inspection Institute of America
314 Main St.
PO Box 4174
Yalesville Wallingford, CT 06492
(203) 284-2311
homeinspi@aol.com

Home Ventilating Institute
30 W. University Dr.
Arlington Heights, IL 60004-1806
(708) 394-0150

International Masonry Institute
823 15th St. NW
Washington, DC 20005
(202) 783-3908

International Wood Products Assn.
4214 Kings St. W.
Alexandria, VA 22302
(703) 820-6696
info@ihpa.org
http//www.ihpa.org

Italian Tile Association
305 Madison Ave., Suite 3120
New York, NY 10165-0111
(212) 661-0435

Kitchen Cabinet Manufacturers Association
1899 Preston White Dr.
Reston, VA 22091
(703) 264-1690

Manufactured Housing Institute
1745 Jefferson Davis Hwy., Ste. 511
Arlington, VA 22202

Maple Flooring Manufacturers Association
60 Revere Dr., Suite 500
Northbrook, IL 60062
(708) 480-9138

Mechanical Contractors Association of America
1385 Piccard Dr.
Rockville, MD 20850
(301) 869-5800

Metal Building Manufacturers Association (MBMA)
2130 Keith Building
Cleveland, OH 44115

Metal Lath/Steel Framing Association Division
600 5. Federal St., Ste. 400
Chicago, IL 60605
(312) 922-6222

Mineral Insulation Manufacturers Association
1420 King St.
Alexandria, VA 22314

National Assn. of Brick Distributors
1600 Spring Hill Rd., Suite 305
Vienna, VA 22182
(703) 749-6223

National Association of Electrical Distributors
45 Danbury Rd.
Wilton, CT 06897
(203) 834-1908

National Association of Home Builders (NAHB)
1201 15th St., NW
Washington, DC 20005-2800
(202) 822-0200

National Association of Home Builders Remodelers Council
1201 15th St., N. W.
Washington, DC 20005-2800
(800) 368-5242 Ext. 216

National Association of Home Inspectors
4248 Park Glen Rd.
Minneapolis, MN 55416
(800) 448-3942
assnhdqs@usinternet.com

National Association of Plumbing-Heating-Cooling Contractors
PO Box 6808
Falls Church, VA 22040
(800) 533-7694
naphcc@naphcc.org
http://www.naphcc.org

National Association of Real Estate Appraisers
8383 E. Evans Rd.
Scottsdale, AZ 85260
(602) 948-8000

National Association of the Remodeling Industry (NARI)
4900 Seminary Rd., Suite 320
Alexandria, VA 22311
(800) 966-7601

National Association of Women in Construction
327 S. Adams St.
Fort Worth, TX 76104-1002
(800) 552-3506

National Concrete Masonry Association (NCMA)
2302 Horse Pen Rd.
Herndon, VA 22071-3499
(703) 713-1900

National Decorating Products Association (NDPA)
1050 N. Lindbergh Blvd.
St. Louis, MO 63132-2994
(314) 991-3470

National Fire Protection Association (NFPA)
1 Batterymarch Park, P.O. Box 9101
Quincy, MA 02269-9101
(617) 770-3000

National Fire Sprinkler Association
Robin Hill Corp. Pk., Rt. 22, Box 1
Patterson, NY 12563
(617) 770-3000

National Forest Products Association
1250 Connecticut Ave. NW, Ste. 200
Washington, DC 20036
(202) 463-2700

National Kitchen and Bath Association (NKBA)
687 Willow Grove St.
Hackettstown, NJ 07840
(908) 852-0033

National Lime Association (MA)
3601 N. Fairfax Dr.
Arlington, VA 22201
(703) 243-5463

National Oak Flooring Manufacturers Association
PO Box 3009
Memphis, TN 38173
(901) 526-5016

National Particleboard Association (NPA)
18928 Premiere Ct.
Gaithersburg, MD 20879-1569
(301) 670-0604

National Pest Control Association (NPCA)
8100 Oak St.
Dunn Loring, VA 22027
(703) 573-8330

National Retail Hardware Assn.
5822 W. 74th St.
Indianapolis, IN 46278-1787
(317) 290-0338

National Roofing Contractors Association
10255 W. Higgins Rd., Suite 600
Rosemont, IL 60018
(800) 323-9545

National Spa and Pool Institute
2111 Eisenhower Ave.
Alexandria, VA 22314-4698
(703) 838-0083
http://www.resourcecenter.com

National Terrazzo and Mosaic Assn.
3166 Des Plaines Ave., Suite 121
Des Plaines, IL 60018-4223
(800) 323-9736

National Wood Flooring Assn.
233 Old Meremac Station Rd.
Manchester, MO 63021
(314)391-5161

National Wood Window and Door Assn.
1400 E. Touhy Ave., Suite 470
Des Plaines, IL 60018-3305
(800) 233-2301
nwwda@ais.net
http://www.nwwda.org

Noise Control Association
680 Rainier Ln.
Port Ludlow, WA 98365
(360) 437-0814

Northern American Insulation Manufacturers
44 Canal Center Plaza, Suite 310
Alexandria, VA 22314
(703) 684-0084

Oak Flooring Institute/National Oak Flooring Manufacturers Association
PO Box 3009
Memphis, TN 38173-0009
(901) 526-5016

Painting and Decorating Contractors of America (PDCA)
3913 Old Lee Hwy. #33-B
Fairfax, VA 22030
(800) 332-PDCA.

Portland Cement Association (PCA)
5420 Old Orchard Road
Skokie, IL 60077
(708) 966-6200

Resilient Floor Covering Institute
966 Hungerford Dr., Suite 12-B
Rockville, MD 20850-1714
(301) 340-8580

Roofing Industry Education Institute
14 Inverness Dr., Suite H-110
Englewood, CO 80112-5625
(303) 790-7200

Safe Building Alliance
655 15th St., N. W., Suite 1200
Washington, DC 20005-5701
(202) 879-5120

Sealed Insulating Glass Manufacturers Association
401 N. Michigan Ave.
Chicago, IL 60611-4212
(312) 644-6610
sigma@sba.com

Sheet Metal and Air Conditioning Contractor's National Association
P.O. Box 70
Merrifield, VA 22116
703-790-9890

Society of Certified Kitchen Designers
687 Willow Grove St.
Hackettstown, NJ 07840
(800) 843-6522

Society of the Plastics Industry (SPI) Spray Polyurethane Foam Division
1801 K. St., N. W., Suite 600K
Washington, DC 20006-1031
(800) 523-6154

Solar Energy Industries Association
122 C St., N. W., Fourth Floor
Washington, DC 20001
(202) 383-2600

Solar Rating and Certification Corp.
122 C St., N. W., Fourth Floor
Washington, DC 20001
(202) 383-2650

Southern Forest Products Association (SFPA)
P.O. Box 641770
Kenner, LA 70064-1700
(504) 443-4464
http://www.southernpine.com

Southern Pine Council
PO Box 641770
Kenner, LA 70064-1700
(504) 443-4464
http://www.southernpine.com

Southwest Research & Information Center (SRI)
P.O. Box 4524
Albuquerque, NM 87106
505-262-1862

Steel Joist Institute (SJI)
1205 48th Ave. N., Ste. A
Myrtle Beach, SC 29577

Steel Window Institute (SWI)
c/o Thomas Assocs., Inc.
2130 Keith Building
Cleveland, OH 44115

Tile Contractors Assn. of America
11501 Georgia Ave., Suite 203
Wheaton, MD 20902
(800) OKK-TILE (655-8458)

Tile Council of America (TCA)
P.O. Box 1787
Clemson, SC 29633-1787
(864) 646-TILE (8453)

Truss Plate Institute (TPI)
583 D'Onofrio Dr., Ste. 200
Madison, WI 53719
608-833-5900

Underwriters' Laboratories (UL)
333 Pfingsten Road
Northbrook, IL 60062

United American Contractors Assn.
85 Central St.
Boston, MA 02109
(617) 357-4470

Vinyl Siding Institute Div. of the Society of the Plastics Industry
1275 K. St., N. W., Suite 400
Washington, DC 20005
(202) 371-5200

Vinyl Window & Door Institute Div. of the Society of the Plastics Industry
1275 K. St., N. W., Suite 400
Washington, DC 20005
(202) 371-5200

Western Red Cedar Lumber Association
1100-555 Burrard St.
Vancouver, BC V7x 1S7
Canada
(604) 684-0266
wrcla@cofiho.cofi.org
http://www.cofi.org/WRCLA

Western Wood Products Association (WWPA)
Yeon Building, 522 SW 5th Ave., Suite 400
Portland, OR 97204-2122
503-224-3930

Women Construction Owners & Executives, USA
4849 Connecticut Ave., N. W., Suite 706
Washington, DC 20008-5838
(800) 788-3548
wcoeusa@aol.com

Bibliography

Marketing Without Advertising
Phillips, Nolo Press

Contractors Contract Kit
CCA

Estimators Form Kit
CCA

Running a One Person Business
Whitmyer, Ten Speed Press

How to Sell Remodeling
Gorodess, Craftsman

Guerilla Marketing
Levinson, Houghton-Mifflin

Word of Mouth Marketing
Wilson, Wiley

Secrets of a Successful Entrepreneur
Dailey, K and A Publications

Web Sites

These web site addresses have information about the topics covered in this course. You will have to look around the site for the information you need. You can benefit from using e-mail to contact people at the site about your questions. In addition, there are usually links to other sites that may be of interest.

If you are a veteran in using the internet, you already know that searching the internet can be frustrating and time consuming. Set out your questions on paper before you go to the internet. Then attempt to stick with these issues in your searching. Refrain from taking side trips until you have your questions answered.

Be sure to check our web site at:

www.Contracting-Academy.com

Best Sellers Special Report Entrepreneur Magazine's BizSQUARE
http://www.entrepreneurmag.com/page.hts?N=327

Canadian Home Builders Association
http://www.buildermanual.com

http://www.magi.com/~homes/

Entreprenuer Magazine
http://www.entrepreurmag.com

Guerilla Marketing Online
http://www.gmarketing.com

Journal of Light Construction Builder's Forum
http://www.bginet.com/jlcforum/index.html

National Association of the Remodeling Industry
http://www.nari.org

National Association of Women in Construction

http://www.nawic@onramp.net (e-mail address)

Northwest Build Net
http://www.nwbuildnet.com
SalesBiz
http://www.salesbiz.com

Sales Doctor Magazine
http://www.salesdoctors.com

Sales Leads USA
http://www.abii.com

The Sales Mall
http://www.salesmall.com

Sales & Marketing Management Magazine
http://www.smmmag.com

Sales Report Smart Business SuperSite
http://www.smartbiz.com/sbs/cats/sales.htm

The Selling Arena
http://www.psahome.com

Tom Hopkins International
http://www.tomhopkins.com

Women Construction Owners and Executives
http://www.wcoeusa@aol.com (e-mail address)

http://www.abuildnet.com

http://www.build.com

http://www.builderbooksite.com

http://www.BuildingOnLine.com

http://www.edgeonline.com

http://www.isquare.com

http://www.smartbiz.com

Remodeling Related

http://www.longrun.onweb.com/remodellinks.html

http://www.probuilder.com/home/home.html

http://www.builderweb .com

Web sites are constantly changing. These sites may change or even disappear. Those sites that are operated by contracting organizations are likely to be the most stable. Your search could lead to other new sites. Let us know if you find a good one.

Index

0 1138 0154847 1
Wentworth - Alumni Library

RECEIVED
ALUMNI LIBRARY

FEB 2 7 2002

Wentworth Institute of Technology
550 Huntington Avenue
Boston, Ma 02115-5998

Date Due

FEB 2 5 2011

BRODART, CO.   Cat. No. 23-233-003   Printed in U.S.A.